L.L. Bean

Hiking and

L.L. Bean
Hiking and Backpacking Handbook

KEITH McCAFFERTY

The Lyons Press

Copyright ©2000 by L.L. Bean

Illustration copyright ©2000 by Tom McCafferty

For photography credits, see page 189

First edition

Printed in Canada

Design and composition by Compset, Inc.

10 9 8 7 6 5 4 3 2 1

Library of Congress Cataloging-in-Publication Data

McCafferty, Keith.
    The L.L. Bean hiking and backpacking handbook / Keith McCafferty.—1st ed.
      p. cm.
    Includes bibliographical references.
    ISBN 1-55821-940-4
    1. Hiking—Handbooks, manuals, etc. 2. Backpacking—Handbooks, manuals, etc. I. Title: LL Bean hiking and backpacking handbook.
    II. Title: Hiking and backpacking handbook. III. L.L. Bean, Inc. IV. Title.

GV199.5.M385 1999
796.51—dc21
                                  99-053860

Contents

Dedication

This book is for my wife Gail, who kept faith when the words wouldn't come. And it is for Joe Gutkoski, who has shrugged into the shoulder straps of his pack as often as most of us have slipped on our shoes, and who doesn't need the words.

Preface

Hiking and backpacking are expressions of our love of nature coupled with a curiosity to explore, to look beyond the curve of the earth visible from our windows and wonder what's there.

Throughout most human history, it was necessary to earn the discovery of backcountry either by walking, paddling a canoe, or by some other manner of travel that demanded both skill and exertion. In the dawn of our new millennium, access to most of the nation's wonders can be bought for the price of a plane ticket and a rental car. The bugle of a bull elk can be heard in Yellowstone National Park from the open window of a hotel room. His majestic antlers can be captured on film with the press of a forefinger, while the car motor idles. By driving a couple hundred miles farther west, someone who photographs that elk at dawn can finish the roll of film before light leaves the sky in the corridor of Idaho's Clearwater River, where fairy-tale larch trees paint feathers of gold against the autumn pines.

Bridging these two areas of natural splendor is a sea of mountains—"as steep as the roof of a house," one member of the Lewis and Clark expedition wrote—that had daunted the Corps of Discovery during the fall of 1805. What takes today's traveler five hours and a choice of CDs to cross took Lewis and Clark a month of riding, walking, and camping, during which they nearly froze to death and perished from hunger.

The contrast between their ordeal and the ease of travel during our age of automation raises questions that some who pick up this book may be asking themselves. Why climb up the flanks of Maine's Mt. Katahdin when more lofty summits are easily conquered by car? Why backpack into Wyoming's Wind River Range when a diamond hitch can secure your duffel to the back of a horse? Why slog through the Everglades when you could stay in an air-conditioned motel and see the alligators from the prow of an airboat?

More than 100 million Americans find satisfactory answers to these questions every year. For the poorer among us, there really isn't a choice. The views gained on horseback come at a much higher price than sights seen on foot, and for the cost of a single night's stay in a hotel, we can backpack for a week or more. Others are attracted by the healthy benefits of the exercise.

Then, too, many understand that only by living outside can we be drawn into the rhythms of nature, where darkness falls with the sinking of the sun instead of the flip of a switch; that only by watching a trout take our fly from the mirrored surface of an alpine lake can we understand its pulse, the ancient struggle for survival that lies beneath the surface of the postcard vistas one obtains behind the wheel of a car. Lying on the earth brings us in closer contact with the spirits of the ancestral hunters who trod this country before us. It gives us a greater appreciation for the traditions we pass down to our sons and daughters and for the inheritance of wild country that satisfies our atavistic passions.

Reflections at the end of the trail. With a vista like this, who needs to go further?

It is vistas like this one that make a trek into the wild worth every step.

The *L.L. Bean Hiking and Backpacking Handbook* examines our impulse to wander while providing simple, clear instruction for anyone whose feet itch to travel beyond the sidewalk. This book contains practical information and reference material that will be of value to those who are at any stage of the trail. But its primary aim is to encourage the beginners, who may be held back by the mistaken notions that hiking and backpacking require a substantial investment in equipment, or that without training in navigation and survival techniques, they will be risking their lives in a trackless wilderness.

The fact is that hiking is walking. The definition changes only after you leave the pavement behind. The benefits of hiking can be reaped by almost anyone.

In his celebrated essay, *Walking*, Henry David Thoreau wrote:

> "Eastward I go only by force; but Westward I go free.... The West of which I speak is but another name for the Wild; and what I have been preparing to say is, that in Wildness is the preservation of the World."

This book is written for all who suspect that their future lies toward the horizon that marks the edge of the Wild, at whatever point of the compass that might be.

There are no roads here, no rumble of car motors, no flumes of exhaust. Only hiker's glory: the roar of the waterfall and a cool mist bathing your face after a hot climb in the sun.

SECTION
I

HIKING

I was fortunate as a child to have a choice of doors that opened to exploration. From our front door rose a steep lawn bordering on a dead-end gravel road. Above this road was our town. For most of the neighborhood children, the impulse for exploration led in this direction, toward the baseball diamonds and street corners, toward the friendships and rivalries of human interaction.

From the door that opened onto our backyard, the country fell away in a series of hickory hills to the valley of the Ohio River. I date my baptism as a hiker to the day my father passed a garter snake into my hands to show me that there was nothing to fear about this beautiful creature. It coiled about my fingers, flicking its forked tongue to taste the air, and when it slipped into the grass, I followed it as far as the edge of the woods. Behind me was our house, and the security of the urban landscape. I hesitated, somehow aware that my life was about to change irrevocably. Then I entered the steep tangle of thorn bushes and trees. Like so many who have been called to footpaths through forest, my heart has never returned.

Those Allegheny foothills grew hazier in the distance, much as the purpose of my early hikes—to catch snakes, to fish for minnows to feed my box turtle, to climb limestone cliffs that looked as imposing as Everest—became less clear the farther I walked. This was *Deliverance* country, where a boy who took a wrong turn might be shot at because a hillbilly spied him near the still above his tarpaper shack, where he could be drafted by unshaven men to fight a forest fire, or go looking for a lost cat and wind up lost himself.

Those memories are like faded snapshots now and my childhood paths have long been lost to thistles and the blades of bulldozers. The trail I sit beside on this autumn afternoon, as I scribble these thoughts, has its terminus high in Montana's Anaconda Pintlar Wilderness, on a tooth of granite that

Hiking is the act of shedding civilization one step at a time. But be careful where you place your feet; in Alpine terrain, stick to trails to avoid damaging fragile vegetation.

rises like a vertebral spur above the backbone of the Continental Divide. In another hour of climbing I will reach a scree slope under the peak, where I hope to photograph a band of bighorn rams. It is a long, long way from Ohio. Yet this is the same trail that began at my back door with the discovery of a snake, 40 years and several thousand miles ago.

Outdoor living is a journey that takes different turns for different people: While one person's legs lead to the mountains, another's will turn to the desert. But I think all of us can agree that no matter where we choose to go, the journey begins in the same way, with the placing of one foot in front of the other. A great deal of metaphysical nonsense has been written about this most basic human act. Some would have you believe that with each turn of the path a new facet of our character is revealed to the sun, so that hiking becomes a safari of self-discovery, even of spiritual rebirth, as we free ourselves from the shackles of urban oppressions and experience personal growth and a new-found sense of worth in the glories of nature.

For a chosen few, salvation may indeed lie at the end of the trail. Such is the belief among Hindus in India, where thousands of pilgrims undertake grueling foot journeys from the scorching plains to the peaks of the Himalayas, in order to immerse themselves in icy pools where the sacred Ganges River is born.

But this is not India and most of us are not religious pilgrims. We hike simply because it is a natural urge, because the genes that prodded our ancestors to wander still linger, like weeds in an otherwise cultivated lawn, to distract our attention from the gridwork of civilization and direct our stride to the remnants of our plains and forests.

Hiking can indeed result in greater self-esteem, as we overcome our fear of the unknown, develop wilderness skills, and come to trust our own judgment at turns in the trail. Hiking encourages contemplation for the solitary, builds camaraderie among companions and serves as a vehicle to cement family bonds that are stretched to thinness by the pressures of school and work, by the omnipresence of television that subverts our very speech and turns family members into conversational strangers.

As a bonus, hiking is healthy; it is probably the most natural and least stressful of aerobic exercises. It is fun, too, reminding you that happiness has much to do with simplicity. Hiking leaves you deliciously tired at the end of a long day, but with a feeling of wholeness, when other exhaustions just leave you weary. Furthermore, hiking strengthens our ties to nature. Hopefully, it encourages us to work toward the preservation of wild areas, so that we might pass this heritage on to our children.

The mind relaxes with the rhythm of hiking. As the clutter and complexity of the life behind us are shed like chaff, we are able not only to think more logically, but to isolate matters of consequence from the trivial worries that so often monopolize our minds. I often find myself calmly composing thoughts on the trail, ordering them so that upon my return I can write them down. Unfortunately, the polished turns of phrase written in my brain prove to be as fragile as dreams; they can no more survive a transition to paper than dreams can be recalled in wakefulness. But the loss is merely one of grammar: The revelations remain. Several of the most important decisions of my life have been made while I had hiking boots on my feet. I think I speak for many others in saying that we go to wilderness not only to escape from the life we left behind, but to gain the perspective of distance, to see things more clearly.

I am writing these words from a position of elevation in the Pintlars, where it is easy to fall victim to your own reverie. If you have yet to take your first step on the trail, such lofty abstractions may not be your concern. Your questions, understandably, are of a more practical nature: What kind of boots do I need to hike? Do I really need a walking staff? A daypack? How many miles

Ridge running on the crest of a reflection. If only altitude was always so easily gained!

can I expect to travel in an hour? These and many other basic considerations are subjects that will be addressed in upcoming chapters.

But before we proceed any further, I must warn you that hiking can be addicting. The impulse to wander through wild country is as ancient as species dispersal and as strong as the tide, and once you take the first step, the trail under your feet never really ends. There is always another rise of land and the urge, no matter how tired you may be, to climb and peer over the top. Hiking is a self-perpetuating passion that even mountain peaks and vesper songs cannot totally conquer. There is always the country that lies beyond. And if it is too late to go there today, perhaps tomorrow.

CHAPTER
1

What to Wear

"Beware of all enterprises that require new clothes."

Henry David Thoreau

While leafing through pages of an outdoor magazine at the grocery checkout stand, I came across an illustration of a well-attired hiker. Arrows led from each article of clothing to text blocks revealing brand name and price; the total, I recall, ran into many hundreds of dollars.

As I waited in line, my mind returned link by link along the chains of memory, until I envisioned two small boys resting atop the pinnacle of Maine's Mount Katahdin. The boys, 7 and 9 years old, were dressed in T-shirts, old corduroys, and sneakers with holes at the toes. When they had left their father and mother at the trailhead, the understanding was they'd walk up the path for a little ways and return. But when you hike, one step does lead to another and the boys had climbed the 5½ miles in a sort of tunnel vision, oblivious to their parent's slow-dawning panic in the parking lot 3,000 feet below.

The other hikers collected at the Baxter Peak overlook were attired in the hiking outfits of the day (the day being in the early 1960s): shirts tucked into knickers, ragg wool socks worn directly over the skin and heavy leather waffle-stompers that could kick a dent in a dinosaur. The Huck Finn outfits of the children drew a few smiles, and a few frowns of concern, too. But the fact is that they had climbed the mountain in more comfort than probably anyone else had that day.

I dredge this story from my memory to raise two points. The first is that times have changed. Not so many years ago, clothes were so itchy and boots

A more tranquil scene is difficult to imagine, but in mountainous country weather can change quickly. Wear layers of clothing that you can peel off or put back on as nature's mercurial moods change.

were so stiff that you had to break your feet into them instead of the other way around. Now the pendulum has swung back toward comfortable apparel, as well as more flexible footwear. The second is that, at least at the entry stage of the sport, hiking requires no special attire, making it not only the simplest of natural recreations, but also the least expensive.

You can hike the vast majority of maintained trails in this country in the shoes and clothes you are wearing as you read this sentence. However, the farther one gets from civilization, the rougher or wetter the trail, the colder the air and, to some degree, the older the hiker becomes, the more one has to ignore Thoreau's warning about enterprises that need new clothes, because clothing and boots made specifically for hiking and backpacking will enable you to walk both more comfortably and safely.

BOOTS AND SOCKS

More than anything else, your enjoyment of the trail depends on the comfort and protection of your feet. Making them happy should be your first concern.

Hiking Socks

For many years, the standard advice given to hikers was to wear two layers of socks—a thin, inner liner of polypropylene or other wicking synthetic, plus a heavier-weight outer sock made of a wool blend. The theory behind the combination is that friction caused by walking takes place between the socks, rather than against your sensitive skin. The *two-sock system* still is preferred by most backpackers, who wear fairly

Trail socks offer extra cushioning at the toe and heel and are a lightweight alternative to the traditional two-sock comb combination of a thin sock liner with a heavy wool outer sock.

The Trouble with Cotton

Stick with wool and synthetics when it comes to clothing your feet. Cotton socks have no insulating value when wet and precious little when dry. They absorb perspiration like a sponge, quickly growing clammy. This combination of wet feet and sticky socks can lead to blisters.

stiff boots and are more likely to suffer from blisters than dayhikers.

Dayhikers have a second option in *sports-blend socks,* which have extra-thick cushioning at the heel, the ball of the foot, and around the toes. These socks are usually a blend of Spandex, nylon polyester, CoolMax, or some other wicking fiber together with acrylic and wool. Sports-blend socks (listed as trail or trekking socks in the L.L. Bean catalogs) are spun very densely and offer more cushioning than old-fashioned rag wool socks that are twice their weight.

Hiking Boots

Americans are suckers for technology. This is something boot manufacturers have not failed to overlook in their advertising blurbs, which lean heavily on techno terminology such as "dual-density," "wing-stabilized," and other such gibberish. Before you become seduced by lingo and find yourself reaching for the mesh-paneled, Achilles'-notched, Tyrannosaurus Rex-soled Denali stompers, ask yourself a very simple question: "Do I really need boots?"

If all you plan to do is dayhike along maintained trails, the answer is probably no. My next-door neighbor Joe Gutkoski bought the very first pair of Nike Air Jordan's to grace our town in 1985 and wore them to climb 12,300-foot Pilot Peak, Montana's highest pinnacle, the very next week. Today, at 72 years of age, Joe Gutkoski has placed Forest Service markers on more peaks in Idaho, Wyoming, and Montana than any other living man. If you were to try to explain to him that his choice of footwear is inadequate for mountaineering, he would pity your ignorance. In fact, Joe's only regret is that he didn't keep those first Air Jordan's in the box. Japanese collectors have been known to pay several thousand dollars a pair.

Today's athletic shoes offer far more support than the old canvas and gum rubber tennis shoes and are perfectly adequate for most hiking. Those marketed as **cross-trainers** are a little stiffer than running shoes and usually have a lug sole or other gripping surface on the sole, making them the best choice.

Trail shoes differ from cross-trainers in having a stiff insole underneath the removable footbed. This makes them more rigid and better suited for rough terrain.

Athletic shoes are fine for dayhiking, but most people who venture off-trail or carry heavy packs will appreciate the greater support of light hikers or backpacking boots.

Lightweight, all-weather Gore-Tex hikers are the most versatile boots for hiking and light backpacking. They will carry you from March to November and from the bottom of the Grand Canyon to the pinnacle of Katahdin.

Trail shoes are low-cut; those marketed as **light hikers** have the same basic construction along with a higher upper for more ankle support.

Light backpacking boots are sturdily constructed for hikers carrying packs weighing up to 30 pounds or so; these boots offer more water resistance than most trail shoes and light hikers. Standard **backpacking boots** are designed to stand up to maximum loads.

There is really no hard and fast rule to refer to when purchasing hiking shoes. Low-cut cross-trainers or trail shoes may be fine for people who have strong ankles and a good sense of balance, but completely unsuitable for oth-

The Microporous Advantage

Many hiking shoes incorporate a microporous membrane such as Gore-Tex, which permits water vapor from perspiration to escape while keeping rain or wet snow out. Microporous membranes are often referred to as breathable fabrics, which is an overly generous definition. Your feet will still become damp, simply because the pores can wick moisture at only a fraction of the rate that it is generated. Still, Gore-Tex liners are well worth the extra 20 to 30 percent they add to cost, because they facilitate construction of exceedingly lightweight boots that you don't have to keep treating with waterproofing wax or mink oil.

ers. Kids usually don't need or want the extra height or weight for trail walking. I'm very sure on my feet but I like the ankle support of higher boots anyway. I also prefer light hikers because the extra height helps keep trail grit from getting into the boot.

Boot Construction

In the interests of lighter weight and cooler feet, the outers of many of today's boots are constructed of Cordura nylon, an extremely tough fabric, or are a leather/Cordura mix. As a rule, the more leather you put into a boot, the heavier and warmer it is, although the addition of a Thinsulate lining can increase the thermal insulation of any boot without adding more than a few ounces. Whether you need extra warmth depends on where you live, but even more so on your particularly body chemistry. Some people's feet stay much warmer than others.

My own preference is for uninsulated, Gore-Tex-lined, all-leather light backpacking boots for three-season walking. They may not hike quite as cool as Cordura boots do, but they offer more ankle support, as well as protection from cactus spines, a consideration throughout much of the West. On cold days, I substitute an all-wool sock for the CoolMax/acrylic blend I typically wear and stuff a couple of flyweight plastic grocery bags into my pack for insurance. By placing the grocery bag between a sock liner and outer sock when I'm backpacking, I can walk with warm feet in temperatures that fall into the teens.

Traction

A boot's traction depends both upon tread design and the material used to make the sole. Boots that have a heavy lug sole afford more traction over a variety of terrain than smooth or lightly ribbed outsoles do. There was a push a decade or so ago among environmentally conscious hikers to have boot makers offer shallower lug designs, to protect fragile alpine areas from being torn up by foot traffic. I had a pair of these politically correct boots and they were okay, but the shallow tread wore out quickly. Another problem was that in order to reach alpine basins, I had to traverse expanses of forests and rocky outcrops where an aggressive tread would have provided surer footing. Perhaps because light-tread designs didn't move off the shoe shelf very quickly, most hiking boots sold today have an aggressive tread. Hikers who remain concerned about abusing alpine meadows should stay on the trail, or else pack along a light pair of tennis shoes for crossing fragile areas.

Getting the Fit

Because shoes are built around foot forms, and each maker uses a slightly different form, some brands will fit you better than others. Don't have your mind set on a brand name when you enter a shoestore.

To fit boots for length, stand in them while wearing the socks you are going to wear along the trail. If you wear orthotics or drugstore footbeds in your street shoes, wear them when trying on the boots. With the boot unlaced, move your foot to the front of the shoe. Stick your forefinger behind your heel. Can you wiggle it just a little? You should have a generous finger's width, but no more.

To order hiking boots from catalogs such as L.L. Bean, have both feet measured at a local shoestore and send or phone in your specifications.

The soles of most hiking shoes have a high carbon content for durability. Soft rubber soles wear out more quickly, but do provide better traction on wet ground or slippery stones. The air-bob design, consisting of small, soft-rubber thimbles, has become first choice among winter campers and hikers who put on a lot of miles over snow. Rubber toe bumpers improve durability and should be considered by anyone who routinely traverses rocky or volcanic terrain that is full of sharp edges.

Boot Care

Leather is skin. It breathes, it absorbs water, and its pores can become clogged with dirt, which breaks down the fibers and shortens its working life. Before treating your boots with conditioner or wax, clean them with a weak solution of water and either a mild dishwashing detergent or Woolite. Run cool water from the spigot and lightly scrub them with a scrub brush. Let them dry completely before treatment. If you want to use a seam sealer, apply it to the seams and allow it to cure before waterproofing the outers.

Both mink oil and leather wax act to repel water. However, mink and other oil-based conditioners soften leather, which is not desirable for most hiking boots. A good water-based wax, such as Nikwax, is better and can be used to waterproof fabric panels on the boot as well as leather.

Rub the wax in thoroughly with your fingers, paying special attention to the folds around tongue gussets and overlapping seams. Remove excess dressing and allow the boots to stand overnight before wearing.

Some hikers warm their boots in an oven, which permits the wax to penetrate the leather more efficiently. But unless you're careful, you'll burn the leather. Err on the side of safety and sit them on a sunny windowsill after treatment or slightly warm them with a hair dryer.

DRESSING FOR THE TRAIL

The layering system of clothing most experts recommend for strenuous outdoor activity has three basic components: an **inner layer** next to the skin that efficiently transfers perspiration to outer garments, an **insulating outer layer** that provides effective dead air space for warmth, and a **shell** that keeps rain out while allowing water vapor created by body heat to pass through and evaporate.

One minute you're in a cold, misty canyon, the next you're basking in sunshine. Dress in layers to accommodate changes in weather and geography.

The Inner Layer

The purpose of clothing is to maintain your body's "thermal equilibrium," a dynamic state of balance in which the heat produced roughly balances heat that is lost through convection, which occurs when the outside air is colder than the body, as well as by evaporation, through sweating. A wicking or absorbing layer next to the skin is essential to maintain this equilibrium, for it transfers water vapor to outer fibers and acts to keep you comfortable and dry. If your skin is wet, it is very difficult to stay warm in anything but the mildest weather.

The passing of vapor from the skin to outer layers of clothing can be accomplished in two ways, by wearing fabrics that *wick* moisture away from the body and pass it to the air or the next clothing layer, or by wearing a fabric that *absorbs* the moisture deep into its fibers, leaving the layer closest to the skin relatively dry.

Synthetic fibers such as polypropylene and polyester are wicking materials; natural fibers including wool and silk are absorbing fibers. Which should you wear?

Wool can absorb about 35 percent of its weight in water before beginning to feel damp and cold against the skin. The drawbacks are that most people find wool itchy and, since wool is such a good insulator, it is unsuitable for warm weather hiking. Another disadvantage of wool is that it dries slowly, making it a poor underwear choice for extended backpacking trips. Wool, however, remains an excellent choice in cold weather, especially when combined with a thin synthetic layer next to the skin to prevent itching.

Like wool, **silk** can absorb up to one third of its weight in water before feeling damp. It offers the benefits of light weight and a luxurious texture that feels almost as good as a lover's touch. However, it requires hand washing and must be laid flat to dry, and it does not dry as quickly as synthetics.

Polypropylene was the first of the synthetics to be touted for its superior wicking properties. Never before had serious hikers been offered a flyweight garment that retained less than 0.1 percent of its weight in water and sucked sweat away from the body as quickly as it was produced. On the other hand, never before had hikers smelled so bad on the trail. Polypropylene absorbed odors, and because it could not be washed in hot water without shriveling, or dried in a dryer without melting, you couldn't get the stink out. Also, the early versions were scratchy. Modern polypro has a smoother texture and can be washed in hot water, somewhat reducing the odor problem.

Today, most base-layer hiking underwear is made of **polyester.** It feels smooth against the skin, can be washed in hot water, and doesn't retain odors.

CoolMax, Thermax, and Thermastat underwear are all based on polyester weaves.

Base-layer clothing is typically offered in three weights: light, medium, and expedition. The heavier weights don't wick as efficiently as the lightest weight, making them poor choices for summer wear or strenuous hiking. Most hikers prefer a lightweight base layer for all but the coldest weather.

The Outer Layer

In hot weather, clothes worn next to the skin also serve as the outer layer. Cotton has been much maligned for its eagerness to soak up sweat, but as an outer layer cotton has a place. Most trail shorts and pants are made of tightly woven cotton or cotton/nylon blends. The addition of nylon adds strength and a measure of wind-resistance to the garment; it also hastens the drying process. Cotton pants and shorts are cool, soft, and comfortable. Sweat is rarely a problem and the large muscles in a hiker's legs generate so much heat during exercise that they seldom become cold. Many hikers wear shorts in near-freezing temperatures.

Two-in-one pants with zip-off legs allow you to start walking on a cold morning in pants, then switch to shorts as the temperature rises. I have long favored them both for hiking and backpacking.

Some hikers prefer stretch trail pants woven with nylon/Spandex or nylon/polyester blends. They are lightweight, pack compactly, and are more durable than pants made of cotton. They wick sweat efficiently and dry in a snap.

Above the waist, sweat can be more of a problem. If you're going to limit hiking to an hour or two, a cotton T-shirt or long-sleeved shirt may be okay, but the wicking ability of a cotton/polyester blend will keep you drier. Polyester-blend shirts also are good choices in hot weather; they wick sweat quickly to the surface, where it can evaporate.

Back and underarm vent panels encourage evaporation and are a particularly good idea in shirts for tropical climates, which often have a tight weave to block ultraviolet radiation.

In cool weather, the two-fold purpose of the outer layer (or layers) is to create dead air space that will trap body warmth and to wick water vapor to the outside fibers, where it can evaporate. No fabrics do this more efficiently than **pile** and **fleece**, which are composed of spun polyester or nylon fibers. Pile has a pronounced nap and looks shaggy. Fleece is a denser fabric with a smooth surface. Both insulate well, wick efficiently while absorbing little moisture, and dry quickly.

A Place for Natural Fibers

Natural fibers have some value as outer layers. Wool shirts and sweaters offer good insulative value and retain a fair measure of warmth when wet. And wool remains the most popular fabric for cool-weather pants, striking a balance between durability, breathability, and comfort across a wide temperature range that synthetics can't match.

Down garments are largely overlooked by today's hikers. True, down is worthless when wet. But nothing packs more compactly, and ounce for ounce, goose down still outperforms the synthetics when it comes to warmth. I pack a down vest on fall hikes as insurance against freak cold snaps, and often find myself shrugging it over my fleece jacket during rest stops or laying it across my legs when I sit to eat lunch.

Pile and fleece are porous, so they offer little resistance to the wind, dramatically reducing their insulative value. You can buy fleece jackets with a built-in wind-resistant lining, but I question the wisdom of this so-called "improvement." One of the great properties of fleece is its breathability, which allows it to be worn comfortably across a broad range of temperatures. Active hikers and backpackers generate a lot of heat and a breeze will feel refreshing in all but the coldest temperatures. It's a relatively simple matter to slip your arms into the sleeves of a Gore-Tex shell during rest stops to prevent chill.

The Shell

Until the advent of Gore-Tex in 1976, people who hiked in rain had two choices: they could forgo raingear and get wet from the outside in, or they could sweat inside a vinyl raincoat and get wet from the inside out. Gore-Tex—a stretchy, untra-thin Teflon membrane developed to graft arteries in surgery—changed that. The pores in Gore-Tex defeated rain because they were smaller than a molecule of water. Yet, being much larger than a molecule of water *vapor,* the pores were still able to permit moisture generated by body heat to pass through to outside air. Thus the first breathable, waterproof clothing was born.

But does it work? Yes, and no. If you sweat hard, Gore-Tex won't pass water vapor as quickly as it is produced, so you'll still get damp. In continuous rain, breathability is reduced because the outside of the garment is partly sealed by water molecules. And in very cold or windy conditions, condensation can form on the inside and even freeze. One of the secrets to staying dry under Gore-Tex and avoiding condensation is to keep base-layer and outside clothing to a bare minimum. Each millimeter of fabric placed between your skin and the Gore-Tex shell reduces its effectiveness.

The microporous advantage: Gore-Tex and other breathable fabrics that repel rain while permitting water vapor from perspiration to escape make hiking safer and more comfortable.

All drawbacks aside, Gore-Tex (and raingear made from other microporous fabrics) is really the only way to go if you hike in country where rain is the rule, rather than the exception.

Alternatives to Gore-Tex include vinyl, coated nylon, or coated polyester. Vinyl raingear is very attractively priced, but it tears easily and isn't practical for anything but occasional use. Nylon or polyester that is coated with polyurethane or PVC is durable and will keep out the rain, although the coating eventually cracks and peels away. Still, if you hike in areas where precipitation is

The Versatile Poncho

Ponchos made of coated nylon or polyester can do double or triple duty as raingear, ground cloths, or tarp shelters. The best ones have a number of grommets for tiedowns (not just at the corners), as well as snaps on either side to fit the poncho closely to the body. Rain does tend to run in through the sleeves when you lift your arms, but ponchos afford a measure of protection to the legs and the material can be draped over a backpack to keep it dry as you hike. Ponchos catch wind like a sail, though, and until you get the hang of them, you'll look like a cat fighting a paper bag as you struggle to get your head and arms in the right places.

rarely a problem, coated synthetics are inexpensive, lightweight, and service-able. You'll get wet if you exercise much in them, but the shell will keep the heat in and you'll stay warm as long as you keep moving.

Hats, Gloves, and Other Clothing Accessories

A warm-weather hat need be nothing more exotic than a baseball cap, al-though it's best to have a brim all the way around that that can be folded down protect your ears and the back of the neck. In tropical climates, a tightly woven straw hat with a wide brim and a crown high enough to provide some air space above the top of the skull is still the best. Above timberline, wear a hat with a chin strap, so you won't lose it in a gust of wind.

Wool is the most popular fabric for cold-weather hats, but fleece dries faster and is warmer for its weight. The old-fashioned balaclava, with a small brim and pull-down face mask, offers the most protection, but many styles are available. In extreme cold, wear a ski mask or a fleece neck gaiter you can pull up over your chin.

Light wool or fleece gloves weigh next to nothing and are good insur-ance against cold, aching fingers. In really cold weather, nothing beats a pair of thick fleece mittens.

Most people associate gaiters with snow, but lightweight, nylon gaiters help keep rain from running down into your boots when you're wearing shorts and are invaluable for keeping nonwaterproof hiking shoes and socks dry during early morning hikes when the grass is frosted or covered with dew.

Clothing Maintenance

Most synthetic underwear, along with fleece and pile, can be washed in warm water (turn garments inside out first). The insulating qualities and wicking abilities of all fabrics tend to diminish when the pores become clogged with dirt and body oils, so keep them clean for best perfor-mance.

Down loses a little loft each time it's washed, even if it is fluffed up at the cool setting in a dryer. Sponge dirt from down clothing rather than tossing it in the washer after each outing. Some compa-

A Touch of Silk

A silk scarf is one of the most versatile and over-looked items of clothing. I start most cold mornings with one wrapped twice around my neck, then wear it loosely with a single knot after warming up. It can be pulled up over my chin against a biting wind, or knotted over my head to keep my ears warm and worn under a felt fedora.

nies professionally clean down. You could inquire about this option at a back-packing or mountaineering store.

Wool loses oil with washing. Except in socks, it is mostly used as an insulating layer and doesn't accumulate a lot of dirt.

Waterproof garments can be damaged by conventional detergents. Nikwax makes special cleaners for breathable, waterproof clothing, as well as for down, polypropylene, and other synthetic fibers.

Climate Control

Clothing Checklist for Hot Weather

- synthetic undershorts and T-shirt
- cotton or nylon shorts or zip-off pants
- cotton, polyester, or polyester/nylon-blend shirt
- broad-brimmed hat
- bandanna to dip in water for evaporative cooling
- synthetic sports-blend socks

Clothing Checklist for the Mountains

- synthetic undershorts
- lightweight, synthetic underwear (top and bottom)
- synthetic zip-off pants or tights
- chamois, microfleece, or wool shirt
- fleece jacket
- waterproof/breathable rain jacket and pants
- lightweight fleece gloves
- baseball cap and fleece or wool hat
- silk scarf
- synthetic sports-blend socks or polypropylene liner socks with wool-blend outer sock

Clothing Checklist for a Rainy Day
(in addition to appropriate synthetic clothing for the temperature)

- waterproof/breathable rain jacket and pants
- poncho

To keep dry during winter stream crossings, use plastic trash bags as emergency waders as these hikers have done while crossing the Flathead River in Montana's Bob Marshall Wilderness.

- waterproof gaiters
- extra socks

Clothing Checklist for Winter Hiking and Backpacking

- synthetic undershorts
- midweight polyester long underwear (top and bottom)
- midweight wool or fleece pants
- wool or microfleece shirt
- fleece jacket
- down vest
- fleece or wool balaclava
- oversize parka
- gaiters
- silk scarf or fleece neck gaiter
- polypropylene sock liners and wool or fleece outer socks

CHAPTER
2

What to Carry

"A good walk requires . . . endurance, plain clothes, old shoes, an eye for nature, good humor, vast curiosity, good speech, good silence, and nothing too much."

RALPH WALDO EMERSON

Hiking poles not only improve balance in rugged terrain, but also ease the load by transferring weight to your shoulders and arms.

When you hike into wild country, your safety depends upon the clothing, food, water, and survival equipment you take with you. But it begins with what you leave behind: a note detailing where you are going and when you should be expected home. If there is no one to leave a message with, place one on the dashboard of your car. Don't overlook signing the register at the trailhead. And don't hike solo until you are confident in your survival gear and navigational skills.

EXTRA CLOTHING

One of the golden rules of hiking is to carry enough extra clothing to survive an overnight stay in case of injury or becom-

Dry Feet Are Happy Feet

Pack extra socks on long dayhikes. Even if your boots stay dry, changing into fresh socks at the halfway point will invigorate your feet and make the last few miles pass more comfortably, with less chance that you will suffer from blisters.

ing lost. Many hikers depend upon a book of matches to provide warmth in case of emergency. However, the unexpected weather changes that may have precipitated your predicament can make fire building difficult.

During the summer at most low altitudes, you might be able to get by with a wool sweater or shirt that maintains some warmth when wet. At higher altitudes or in desert areas, where temperatures can plummet precipitously after sunset, it's a good idea to pack along a fleece jacket and warm cap.

A poncho or rain jacket should be part of your kit, too, especially during wilderness hikes. For shorter trips or in typically dry climates, it may be enough to pack a couple of heavy-duty plastic trash bags. You can cut holes for your head and arms in one and wear the other as an improvised skirt. Combined with a brimmed hat, you'll stay surprisingly dry on the walk back to the car.

FOOD AND WATER

Hikers lose a great deal of fluid through sweating and rapid breathing, especially in dry air at higher altitudes. Urinary output also increases with altitude, cold, and exertion. For these reasons, it's important to stay well hydrated. Slacking your thirst with a few sips from a water bottle during rest stops isn't enough. Drink lots of fluids *before* you start to walk and drink at least a quart of water for every two hours you hike on the trail. Drink more in very hot weather, whether or not you are thirsty.

Sports drinks such as Gatorade, which are high in carbohydrates and electrolyte supplements, contain sugars in a form the body can absorb quickly. They will boost your energy level, but should not be considered a substitute for water, which you need to eliminate waste buildup.

Carry water in liter- or quart-sized bottles with secure lids, available from any outdoor store. Wide-mouthed containers are better during cold-weather hikes, when ice buildup can clog bottles with small openings.

Trail food should be heavy in carbohydrates, but not to the point that fats and proteins are entirely neglected. Good sources of carbs include dried fruits, bagels, rice cakes, granola bars, and most energy bars. Make sure you have a bag of peanuts, a few sticks of jerky or other meats for protein, and

Hikers need extra calories to keep going. Snack frequently to provide your bloodstream with the sustained release of sugars it needs to maintain your energy level.

perhaps a cube of cheese for fat. Beware of "power bars" that are high in fructose corn syrup; to be properly digested, they require lots of water.

Nibble frequently during hikes rather than taking a single lunch break. Your stomach will be less likely to cramp and your body will absorb the food more easily in small quantities.

HIKING POLES

A pair of hiking poles not only aid greatly in balance, but relieve the burden on lower extremities by transferring weight to your shoulders and arms. Most hiking poles have telescoping sections that can be adjusted for differences in terrain. Some have shock absorbers; I've seen a few with compasses built into the handle. You can find hiking poles at tonier outdoor sports stores and mail-order houses (see Reference section), but be aware that they can be pricey.

Lightweight cross-country ski poles are an option for the budget-minded hiker and often can be purchased at garage sales or ski swaps for a few dollars.

A pair of good stout sticks works, too, and won't set you back a dime.

Except for an aluminum fly-rod case, I seldom use a walking stick during dayhikes, but have become a believer in them for extended backpacking trips, where a top-heavy load tends to put you off-stride. One walking stick is all you need for improved balance; two, however, are much better for taking weight off your joints.

A hiking staff has many uses aside from the obvious. In snake country, it sweeps the grass in front of you to prompt rattlesnakes into buzzing, reducing your chance of stepping on one accidentally. It is your third leg during river crossings, can be extended for a companion to hold onto during a steep climb, knock snow from overhead bushes before you duck underneath, hold briars to the side of the trail while your tender flesh passes by, or prop up your pack so it makes into a backrest. You also can use your staff to lift a pot off a campfire, stir ashes, or rough up the ground cover where you rested so that all signs of human presence are erased.

EMERGENCY GEAR

When I was a boy, I hopped freight trains that whistled out into the Ohio countryside, then jumped off where the trestle bridged Cross Creek. Besides a fishing rod, I took nothing on these trips but a wandering spirit and the clothes on my back. I drank from the creek, went without food, and after making a few dozen casts for smallmouth bass, I'd hike seven or eight miles through the foothills to get back home, looking for snakes along the way and climbing the last ridge in time to see fireflies winking under the willow tree in our back yard.

I was so smart back then that I knew I'd never die. Today, I am not so certain about half the things I thought I knew, but something I have learned is that a cavalier attitude toward the dangers of walking in wild country without survival gear can have serious repercussions.

Dayhiker's Survival Kit

All hikers should carry a small survival kit in case of emergencies, no matter how short their walks are or how many other people they are likely to see along the trail. The kit should include:

- waterproof matches
- butane cigarette lighter
- flint and steel
- solid fuel cubes or other fire-starting material
- plumber's or backpacker's candle (they burn longer than regular candles)
- emergency space blanket (the kind that is sewn in the shape of a sleeping bag is the most efficient at conserving body warmth)
- 2 compasses
- sunscreen

- sunglasses
- insect repellent
- small medical kit (many outdoor stores sell these or they can be mail-ordered through L.L. Bean)
- a sheet of Spenco 2nd Skin and a square of moleskin for blisters
- personal medications
- iodine tablets for water purification
- flashlight with spare bulb and batteries (wrap the barrel with a few turns of electrical tape and a few turns of duct tape, so the tape will be available if needed for repairs)
- shrill whistle
- 10-feet of bright orange marking tape to mark a trail in case you become lost
- knife
- roll of dental floss* with a heavy-duty needle taped inside the lid
- folded square of aluminum foil (foil has a dozen and one uses, including catching rainwater, cooking trout, covering a cup or pot, or even providing a heat-reflecting foundation to build an emergency fire on in snow country)
- Energy bar
- Toilet paper

This sounds like a lot of gear, but in fact all of these items except the sunglasses fit inside a 6″ × 4″ zippered Cordura pouch that you wear on your belt. Alternatively, you can place survival gear inside a heavy-duty reclosable plastic bag or small stuff sack and keep it in a daypack or fanny pack. Because hikers sometimes become separated from their packs, I advocate the belt pouch—it stays with you at all times.

Always carry strike-anywhere wood matches—preferably the windproof type that burn with a furious flame—in addition to safety matches, which require a chemical reaction between the matchhead and the rough strip on the side of the box to ignite. If the strip becomes tattered or soggy, you're out of luck.

Store matches in a 35mm film canister or other waterproof match container (a reclosable plastic bag works, too). It's also wise to carry a small flint and

---

*Dental floss makes an excellent strong thread; I once used to it to stitch up my wife's pack after a bear had ripped it apart while we were backpacking in Yosemite National Park.

One of the hiker's most important survival tools is a good orienteering compass with a straight edge that can be used to plot bearings on topographic maps.

steel to insure a spark under the worst possible conditions. Remember, hypothermia is the number-one cause of death for people in the outdoors. A reliable spark and a few fire-starting paraffin cubes are the best two ounces of prevention you can pack.

A top-grade orienteering compass that adjusts for declination and can be aligned with a map to draw bearings is a must for any serious hiker. You also should purchase one of those little, liquid-filled ball compasses that clip onto your shirt. Although not adjustable for declination, they give you magnetic north at a glance. By referring to your compass every few minutes, rather than only after you become lost (which is the tendency when the compass is zipped away in a pack), you constantly orient yourself with regard to prominent landmarks and are less likely to become turned around. A person with a good sense of direction is simply one who keeps track of where he or she is going.

When it comes to knives, the safest kind is a folding knife with a lock-back blade that can't close on your fingers. However, Swiss Army knives are difficult to resist. The miniature tools actually do work, and models that include scissors and tweezers come in handy when you need to remove splinters, trim your nails, or mend a part of your kit with needle and thread.

Our eyes are among the most vulnerable organs in our bodies, but few hikers give any thought to protecting them from ultraviolet (UV) radiation or the tree branches and brush that overhang trails. All hikers should seriously consider buying glasses with clear, shatter-resistant polycarbonate lenses for protection against corneal scratches. At high altitudes or in bright sunlight, it's important to wear lenses that offer 100-percent UV protection. Polarized lenses cut glare from water and are nice if you plan to fish. Some sports glasses come with interchangeable clear and tinted lenses to cover both bases.

Near the top of the list in flashlights is the Mini-MagLite that runs on two AA cell batteries. It is water-resistant, lightweight, and has a recessed cavity that houses a spare bulb. Mine hasn't once failed in 15 years of continuous usage. An accessory I highly recommend, the Bite-Lite, slips over the end so you can hold the flashlight in your teeth, leaving both hands free to prepare dinner or tie knots. An alternative is a headband accessory with a sleeve to hold the light.

Additions to the Survival Kit

On hikes that stray from established trails or penetrate into wild country, it's also a good idea to pack the following items:

- trail guide
- topographic map and pencil to plot compass courses
- emergency strobe, smoke bomb, or signal flare to alert rescuers of your position in case you are injured or become lost
- 6-foot square of clear plastic Visqueen or coated nylon tarp
- nylon cord (30 to 50 feet of parachute [550] cord)
- 12″ × 12″ square of closed-cell pad to sit on during rest stops

A trail guide and topo map provide cheap insurance against becoming lost and a tarp can be pitched as an impromptu shelter if you have to overnight unexpectedly in inclement weather. Also, when the tarp is converted into a solar still for collecting water (see Chapter 11), it can save your life if you become lost in the desert.

Braided nylon "parachute" cord, also known as 550 cord (it is 550-pound test), has many uses, some of them hidden in its core, which is comprised of smaller braided nylon strands. The smallest-diameter strands can be unraveled to provide a strong sewing thread or fishing line; the medium-sized ones can be threaded through the hole in your knife handle to keep it from becoming lost, used as a lanyard for your compass, for general gear repairs, or, in dire circumstances, as a bow string or snare for catching rabbits and other small game for food. Looped over a tree limb, the cord will pull a food bag out of a bear's reach. Parachute cord can be used to raise or lower your pack along steep inclines or provide security to a companion on a tricky part of the trail; however, it is *not* an adequate substitute for climbing rope. Parachute (550) cord also makes an excellent shoelace. It is sold by the foot in outdoor sports stores and Army/Navy stores. Thirty feet of cord weighs about a pound.

Use common sense and customize the survival kit to the climate and country you'll be hiking.

Optional Gear

Depending upon the nature of your hikes and personal interests, you might also consider packing:

- camera
- fishing equipment
- field guides (to help identify wildflowers, reptiles, birds, etc.)
- binoculars
- notepad and pencil

When I first started hiking, carrying a camera that took decent photographs was equivalent to putting a brick in your pack. Today, you can find any number of excellent point-and-shoot 35mm cameras that weigh in the neighborhood of half a pound. The weather-resistant models tend to weigh a few ounces more but stand up much better, not only to the occasional raindrop but also to rough handling or an accidental fall.

Hikers who like to fish have a couple of options. Take-down pack rods tend to cost half again as much as two-piece fishing rods, but you can stuff them inside a daypack and forget about them until you reach the lake, leaving both hands free. I once made a four-piece fly rod that fit inside the aluminum tubes of an external frame backpack. If you do opt for a take-down rod, I advise against the combination fly/spin rods. They are cheaply made and do a poor job at either type of casting. The alternative to pack rods is to carry a full-size two-piece rod and use a lightweight aluminum rod case for a walking stick.

Field guides, such as those in the Peterson and Golden Guide series, are offered on a variety of subjects, from bird and reptile identification through mineralogy and star gazing. These books, along with the Pocket Guides, also are available in condensed booklets, which are easy to pack but lack detailed descriptions of all species. The smaller, pocket-sized guides offer a good entree to the natural world for children.

Compact binoculars open up a world of vision along the trail. They not only permit a closer look at birds and animals, but gather light, enabling the viewer to see more clearly at dawn and twilight than is possible with the naked eye. Binoculars come in various powers such as 7×35, 8×25, and 9×40. The first number denotes the magnification. The second number refers to the size in millimeters of the objective lens, which determines how much light the glass can gather. Generally speaking, an 8×40 binocular will gather more light than an 8×32 binocular, and give you a lot clearer look at wildlife in periods of low light. The tradeoff is that larger objective lenses translate into greater weight.

Unless you are a very serious birder, a compact binocular in the 8×30 power range is adequate, offering a good balance of power and light-gathering capability, without being too heavy. Higher powers are tempting, but the greater the magnification, the more difficult it is to hold binoculars steady enough to keep the image from trembling.

Binoculars not only bring birds and animals into closer focus, but gather light to make viewing more enjoyable in the morning and evening, when wildlife is most active.

To record your field notes or thoughts, carry a small notebook or sketch pad. More expensive versions with waterproof paper are a good idea for extended treks or wet climates.

DAYPACKS AND FANNY PACKS

As soon as you go beyond short dayhikes and start adding food, water or much extra clothing to the basic survival kit, you're faced with the decision of where to put it. There are two choices: the fanny pack and the backpack (full-sized packs will be discussed in Chapter 6).

Fanny packs are extremely popular and come in many designs, most with special water-bottle holsters. Some incorporate lash tabs or compression straps for securing extra clothing to the outside. Fanny packs offer several advantages over traditional backpacks. These small packs cling to the small of your back, so they don't scrape against overhanging tree limbs or get in the way when you must pass through a narrow place in the trail. Moreover, they don't make your back sweat. Nor do they shift your center of gravity and throw you off-balance, as taller packs sometimes do.

On the down side, fanny packs can't carry as much gear. This is a mixed blessing, for just as work expands to fill the time allotted to it, gear tends to

The hiker's choice: A daypack (left) carries more gear, but a fanny pack (right) is lighter and won't make your back sweat.

expand into every available square inch of a pack. Carry a big pack and your inclination will be to fill it. The other drawback of fanny packs is that the weight tugs at your back. That isn't a problem if you keep the load light, but if you carry more than six or seven pounds, you'll wish you had shoulder straps to bear the brunt of some of the weight and position it over your hips.

A backpack evens out weight distribution and can accommodate more gear, especially bulky items. That's important, because the fleece jackets, down vests, ponchos, and closed-cell pads that add comfort and safety to a long hike don't weigh much but do take up considerable space.

The simplest backpacks, sometimes referred to as rucksacks, are soft-sided and do not have waist belts. Children all over this country put 15 pounds of books into them and tote them to school as if they were carrying packs full of goose down. But most serious hikers would not carry a pack across the street unless it had a wide, fully padded waist belt to transfer most of the load to the hips. A chest strap also helps in balance and load distribution by pulling the pack closer to your back.

The internal-frame pack, with hidden stabilizers made of plastic or aluminum, is the most suitable design for hiking and light backpacking. Some of the better models have full-length carbon fiber stays that flex with your movement and attach directly attach to the hip belt, which aids in weight transfer. Backpacks with adjustable stays that can be custom-fitted to the contours of your back or that offer several choices of cant— the angle at which the stays attach to the belt—also are available, but at a price, naturally. How important these bells and whistles are depends on your budget, fitness level, and the weight you are carrying. The heavier the load, the more crucial the fit.

Dayhiking packs range in capacity from about 1,000 to 3,500 cubic inches. Larger models are better if you plan to do any overnighting.

The Ten-Percent Solution

How much weight you pack on dayhikes depends largely on weather and terrain. In cold climates, where you need extra clothing, or in the desert, where you may pack up to eight pounds of water, your pack naturally will weigh more. But under favorable conditions, you ought to be able to keep the weight down to ten percent of your body weight, while still packing enough food and survival gear to play it safe. A 120-pound woman should be able to carry 12 pounds without fatigue, once she's in condition. Add much more than that and you reach a point where it becomes difficult to walk freely and ignore the load on your back. Your mind focuses on the next rest stop, while enjoyment along the trail begins to suffer.

A sunlit trail through a grove of young aspens: a backpacker's paradise.

Other options you should consider include full-size backpacks with de-tachable hoods that convert into fanny packs, or packs that consist of two parts—an upper section that converts into a rucksack and a lower section that converts into a fanny pack. Some of the most innovative designs are made for hunters, who need a full pack to haul gear to a base camp and tote meat, but prefer to hunt with a light daypack or fanny pack. These packs are worth checking out and can be found in sporting goods stores and mail-order houses that cater to outdoorsmen.

CHAPTER 3

Hitting Your Stride

"Afoot and light-hearted I take to the open road,
Healthy, free, the world before me,
The long brown path before me leading
wherever I choose."

WALT WHITMAN

Growing up in 1960s, I walked to school in the mornings. My route started on a gravel road and it ended on pavement, but for a quarter mile I trod a path that hunted down limestone cliffs and cut through dense brush before emerging on Cherry Avenue. Hiking was a daily habit— one borne of necessity rather than choice.

Today, most kids ride the bus or are driven to school. We live faster lives and seldom downshift long enough to consider that our legs, not being powered by fossil fuels, actually remain a viable mode of transportation.

To unlock the joys of hiking, you must first wrench your brain away from its obsession with the nervous ticking of the twenty-first century and grow comfortable with the natural rhythms of your body. You must learn to be satisfied with going nowhere in a hurry. The way to accomplish this isn't by driving 50 or 150 miles twice a summer, slamming the car door, and hustling to the peak of Old Baldy and back. All you will discover at the end of that trail are sore feet and a residue of anxiety, reversing the gradual winding down of gears to restore the frantic and disjointed thoughts, worries, and obligations you had hoped the climbing would erase.

Instead, you need to rediscover the habit of walking in the course of everyday living. That is the most natural and quickest way to tone the muscles you

Autumn aspens are a hiker's gold that can't be mined by anyone who just sits behind the wheel. You have to exercise your legs to appreciate the beauty of a stand of aspens in Colorado's Maroon Bell Range.

will need to hike in more rugged terrain, as well as to ease back into the pace that our blood pressure tells us is the right way to live.

GETTING READY TO HIKE

Most of us are too entrenched in our own individual way of walking to make significant changes as soon as we take up hiking. However, it's important to wear shoes that fit our feet and are suited to the terrain we'll be traveling over. It's also important to correct problems resulting from flat feet or pronation that alter stride and place undue stress on ankle, hip, and knee joints. Those who are young may need to make no adjustment before hitting the trail, but custom-made orthotics and off-the-shelf arch supports or footbeds that re-place your boots' removable insoles can make a big difference in the way stress is distributed to your body during hiking. If you experience discomfort or notice markedly uneven wear on the soles of your shoes, seek the advice of a podiatrist, physical therapist, or chiropractor before you undertake any strenuous hikes.

Exercise

The best way to train for any sport is to exercise in a way that simulates the activity. For a hiker, that means walking. A teenage girl may be able to hike her age in miles without training—the problem with children of either sex is more often one of motivation than physical conditioning—but if you are older and have led a sedentary life, you'll need to start with shorter distances. Wear loose, comfortable clothing and put one foot in front of the other. That's all there is to it, really. Slowly increase the distance you walk, making sure you don't push too hard in a short period of time.

Stretching

Most physical health professionals don't recommend stretching cold muscles. However, it is a good idea to perform a few simple stretches the first time you stop to rest or admire the view, after your leg muscles have warmed up. Stretching will enable you to reach the full range of motion in your joints and will reduce the risk of injuries caused by straddling blow-downs, hopping creeks, or other activities that strain leg and back muscles.

Simple stetching exercises for the calf and quadriceps can easily be per-formed in the field using a rock, backpack, or tree trunk for support (see fig-ures on page 36 and 37). Propping your outstretched leg on a handy rock or log and bending from the waist can stretch hamstring muscles at the back of the upper leg. Never stretch muscles to the point of pain. When you feel a dull ache in the muscle being exercised, hold the stretch for 10 seconds, then release and repeat the exercise with the other leg. Stretching exercises per-formed a couple of days a week will maintain existing flexibility; you will have to stretch your muscles three to five days a week to improve the range of motion.

People who have sedentary lifestyles may need a more vigorous stretching program to restore flexibility to tendons and muscles that have shortened af-ter years of inactivity. The best way to do this is by using a two-person tech-nique called *proprioceptive neuromuscular facilitation* (PNF), which is based on

You can use your pack or lean against a tree trunk for support while you stretch your calf muscles.

contraction and relaxation principles. In PNF, your partner applies steady pressure at the outer limit of your range of motion. After 10 seconds, you contract the muscle being stretched, pushing back against the steady pressure applied by your partner. After another 10 seconds, relax the muscle. Your partner should then be able to apply pressure and extend your range of joint motion another three degrees or so. This sequence is repeated three or four times, which should result in about a 10-degree gain over your initial range of motion. Because you have to rely on a knowledgeable partner to know when to ease off the pressure, PNF stretches are riskier than static ones. They are, however, the best way to improve joint flexibility.

Aerobic Benefits of Hiking

Hiking is often touted as a great aerobic exercise. It can be, but in order to significantly increase cardiovascular endurance—the heart and lungs' capacity to take in oxygen and deliver it to the cells—you need to keep your heart rate at an elevated level for 20 to 30 minutes at least three times a week. If you do other aerobic exercises to maintain fitness, this may be of little concern. Why interrupt your hike to look at your watch and monitor your pulse, when your purpose in the woods is to listen to the heartbeat of the Earth?

Stretch and strengthen the quadriceps muscles at the front of your thighs to help prevent knee injuries.

But if walking is your only exercise or you are working toward a goal, such as a week-long hike along a leg of the Appalachian Trail, then it's important to know how long and at what pace you must walk to make aerobic gains.

Heart rate is the most precise indicator of exercise intensity. To estimate this rate while hiking, place two fingers against the artery just under the side of your jaw or on the inside of your wrist, count the pulse for six seconds and multiply by ten.

The purpose of aerobic exercise is to bring your heart rate into a target zone—calculated at 50 to 85 percent of your maximum heart rate—and keep it there for at least 20 minutes before cooling down. To determine your maximum heart rate, subtract your age from 220.

At the beginning of aerobic training, shoot for lifting your heart rate into the low end of the target zone. As you get into better condition, gradually bring your heart rate into the higher range. For example, a 40-year-old woman's maximum heart rate would be 180. The low end of her target zone would be half that rate, or 90 beats a minute. The upper end of her range would be 153 beats a minute.

You'll have no difficulty reaching the target zone if your hikes take you uphill, but a leisurely walk may not do the trick. If you can sing the aria to *Rigoletto* without feeling winded, you need to go faster.

Never be discouraged into thinking you are either too old or out of shape to reap the rewards of exercise. Studies indicate that a three-month aerobic fitness program will typically increase cardiovascular endurance by 20 percent. Considering that beyond the age of 25, aerobic fitness declines about 1 percent a year, you should be able to turn back your biological clock by about 20 years. The word that springs to mind is rejuvenation.

Strengthen Those Hiking Muscles

Strength training benefits hikers and backpackers in three ways: by improving muscular power, which is needed to carry heavy loads; by increasing muscular endurance, so that you can walk farther without fatigue; and by

A

B

C

D

*Figure A. Leg Pull-in (lower abdominals). Sitting on the edge of a bench (in the field, use a rock or log), exhale and extend legs parallel to the floor. Bend your knees and inhale while lifting your upper thighs toward your stomach. Repeat. For balance, grasp the log or bench behind your buttocks. **B.** Back Extension (back and spinal support muscles). Lie on the ground with your legs straight and your arms folded against your chin. Raise your upper torso by rolling up your head and neck. Hold 5 seconds. Repeat. **C.** Bent Knee Sit-up (mid and upper abdominals). Sit on the ground with legs flexed and soles flat against the ground. With hands clasped behind your head, pull up to position indicated in the illustration, then lower back to floor. Repeat. **D.** Quadriceps Lift. Sit on bench, rock, or stump with both feet on the ground, grasping your seat for support. Lift left leg to horizontal. Hold 5 seconds. Repeat on opposite side. As muscles grow stronger, introduce resistance with ankle weights or an elastic band.*

slowing—even reversing, in some cases—the loss of bone density that accrues with age. The latter is extremely important for aging baby boomers, particularly women, who tend to lose bone mass at a more accelerated rate than men.

The exercises illustrated in Figures A, B, and C might be looked upon as the bare minimum one can get away with to maintain the abdominal and spinal support muscles, without which the vertebrae of your back would collapse like a stack of dominos. Medical authorities attribute the majority of pains and aches that detract from the enjoyment of life and can make even simple walks of a mile or two miserable to weak, imbalanced muscles of the lower trunk.

The exercise shown in Figure D develops the quadriceps muscle in the front of the thigh. This is arguably the most important muscle for hikers to strengthen, because it controls how hard and accurately your feet strike the ground during walking. The stronger your quads, the less jarring your stride is to your knees.

In order to significantly increase bone density and muscle strength, you must introduce greater resistance into your exercises than your body alone can provide. That can be done with elastic tubing, machine weights, or free weights, such as barbells and dumbbells. Many fitness professionals recommend free weights, because they exercise the smaller, helping muscles as well as the stabilizing muscles that support larger muscle groups. It is the balance of strength between the lifting muscles and the stabilizers that enables you to support and balance a heavy backpack while hiking.

Having struggled for many years to maintain a training regimen on my own, I encourage anyone who seriously wants to build stronger muscles and better bones to join an athletic club, where you can stay motivated by working out alongside like-minded people.

FINDING YOUR PACE

How far can I hike in a day? How long will it take us to reach the peak? These are the kinds of questions people new to hiking ask at campfires and trailheads, and to which there are no simple answers.

A hiker's pace depends upon the speed and length of his stride and would be easy to calculate if he was walking on a trail that offered firm footing and a straight path through the woods without any appreciable elevation change. Most hikers can maintain pace of 2 to 3½ miles per hour on level ground. But trails do climb and fall, and when you add a number of other variables, such as altitude, trail condition, weather, number and duration of rest stops, places

No matter which trail you choose, the miles you cover seem longer than the distance marked on a map. Some hikers believe forest employees take a mischievous pleasure in marking trails as shorter than they really are!

where you must use caution due to insecure footing, drop-offs, or the relative likelihood of encountering grizzly bears (a matter of no little concern in my part of the country), the same hiker might cover as little as half a mile in an hour, or as many as five miles.

I once mapped out a long dayhike in New York's Adirondack State Park that would take a companion and me up and down four peaks, starting with Mount Marcy, the park's highest mountain. The route did not seem overly ambitious. The famed conservationist Bob Marshall, who founded the Wilderness Society and for whom Montana's Bob Marshall Wilderness is named, had in the summer of 1932 climbed 14 Adirondack peaks, including Mount Marcy, on a hike that lasted 19 hours and ascended a total of 13,600 feet. If Marshall could do that, I figured my friend Gigi and I could do a third of the route if we started early enough.

We were on the trail, in pouring rain, at 5 A.M. Slipping and sliding with every step, we barely had enough time to conquer Mount Marcy and return to the trailhead by dark.

I recall this story to illustrate how difficult it is to predict the time it will take to reach trail destinations, and how often even veteran hikers attempt to cover more distance than it is reasonable to achieve.

Start small. A hike of a half mile or so is far enough if you are unaccustomed to the exercise. Warm up by starting slowly, then gradually build to a comfortable pace. Don't bend forward at the waist or lock your knees; walk erect. On uneven terrain, take short steps that don't disrupt balance. Where the trail climbs and you have to step up to reach the next foothold, be careful not to bend your knee beyond a 45-degree angle. Be particularly cautious going downhill, where the weight of your body places more strain on your muscles and your knees and ankles. Until you have strengthened the muscles that aid in balance, you will be more susceptible to ankle sprains, shin splints, or knee dislocations than conditioned hikers. A strength training program can narrow the gap, but not overnight. If you are prone to injury, wear supportive boots with heel cups that keep your feet from turning and uppers that are high enough to offer ankle support.

HIKING WITH COMPANIONS

Every person has a natural walking pace at which he feels most comfortable. When a hiker forces himself to hike faster, his feet no longer strike the earth in a relaxed rhythm. Hurrying, he takes chances in tricky terrain, perhaps trips on a tree root and falls down. Forced to walk at a slower pace than normal, he must either shorten his natural stride or alter his gait so that his legs move more slowly. He becomes like a car with a poor automatic transmission, cruising down the road at a speed that falls between gears. His motor lurches into second gear, falls back into third, then lurches again. With his body rhythm out of synch, the hiker becomes distracted and anxious. This can lead to trail injuries, or at least to irritated companions.

How then, can one hike contentedly and safely with people who walk at different paces?

I was faced with that dilemma in Montana's Glacier National Park one summer, when I organized a hike for 11 family members who ranged in age from 12 to 67. After trying to keep the group together for the first half-mile, it became apparent that no one was having fun. The solution was simple: allow people to assemble themselves into several groups and proceed at their own pace. I went ahead with the three boys. My sister-in-law, Shelly, headed the next group, which included two younger girls. My wife, Gail, and her brother lagged farther back, content to walk slowly in order to talk and catch up on family news. The oldest members of the group, Gail's mother Joanne and her Aunt Carol, completed the lower leg of the trail, but when it began to climb they turned back and took an easy loop to the trailhead, where they rested

Strides and stamina differ. Usually it's better to let hikers in your party break into small groups that proceed at a pace most comfortable for them rather than force everyone to hike together.

and awaited our return. As a result of our mutual agreement to split into smaller groups, everyone had a rewarding experience.

Unfortunately, I also have been on hikes where slower walkers, motivated by pride or fear of being left behind, struggled to keep apace, while the members with longer legs ignored their plight and pressed on relentlessly. Hiking is not a competition. If the pace of your companions is too fast for you, speak up.

When hiking off-trail or through grizzly country, it is wise to stick together. Then it falls to the faster hikers in the group to slow their pace down. But on many trails, it is perfectly acceptable for one or more to walk ahead, as long all members of the party are comfortable with the plan and have come to an understanding regarding rendezvous points up the trail.

HIKING WITH CHILDREN

Kids can be great hiking companions. They are infinitely curious about the natural world, but their attention spans are short, whereas trails tend to be long. There's little to be gained by pushing them faster or farther than they want to go. Pack a guidebook about insects, birds or reptiles and stop often to explore the world at your feet or life in the treetops. Bring binoculars to spot birds and deer. Look at animal tracks. Use an interesting destination, such as a waterfall, as a motivational tool.

When they begin to show signs of impatience or fatigue, stop for a few minutes and dole out snacks. Ask them what song they'd like to sing. A good sing-along can be worth another half mile of trail. So can the gift of a walking stick strung with bear bells, even in places where there aren't any bears.

Stay sensitive to mood swings and be prepared to scale back the length of your hike when children become tired or cranky. One of the most important lessons my wife and I learned about hiking with our own children was that kids who seem eager to hike one day may be adamantly against the idea the next. So it helps to have a flexible schedule.

At what age can you start kids hiking? Native American women packed their infants in papooses as tribes followed bison herds across the plains and moved to seasonal camps, and there is no reason why you can't do the same.

In fact, babies are among the best hikers, though admittedly ones who never place their feet on the ground. Choose a backpack carrier with a fully-padded hipbelt, which will help distribute the load on longer hikes. Infants less than four months old are better off in a front carrier; their weak neck muscles can't support their heads in a backpack carrier.

Toddlers can undertake short nature walks and they are fascinated by all that goes on around them, but don't expect to get anywhere fast. Don't expect to get anywhere at all, for that matter. You'll probably wind up carrying them farther than they walk.

Four- to six-year-olds can easily undertake hikes of a mile or two, but stamina doesn't really kick in for most kids until they are seven or eight. That's when you can begin to

Choose a child carrier with a rain cover that will protect your child against burning sun or inclement weather. A retractable stand to keep the carrier upright during rest stops is a great feature, but make sure the stand is on level ground to prevent tipping.

Fly fishing offers children a glimpse into the working order of nature—big fish eat little fish, little fish eat aquatic insects and so on. A rod also is a motivational tool, for miles pass much more quickly when the end of the trail offers the promise of a trout.

take them on the longer dayhikes that you would choose for yourself. It's a critical age, however, where a few experiences of being pushed to hike too far or in bad weather can sour their enthusiasm for hiking for the rest of their lives. It helps if you encourage them to develop a hobby, such as photography or fishing, which gives them something to look forward to besides walking.

By the time kids become teenagers, they either like hiking or they don't. But even if they do, they may balk at the prospect just because it was your suggestion, or because their social lives have become more important to them than adventures with their parents. Asserting independence is a natural part of growing up and we must accept the fact that we may lose our hiking companions for a few years during the process. One trick I've learned with my own teenage children is to have them invite a friend on our hiking trips. That way they don't have to put up with the inferiority of adults all by themselves.

NEGOTIATING STEEP TERRAIN

Many of our nation's most scenic hiking trails wind among rugged mountains or seaside cliffs. You don't have to be a mountaineer to enjoy this country. However, in some places it may be necessary to do a little rock scrambling, while in others the trail may skirt steep drop-offs where a slip could be fatal.

The cardinal rule of climbing a steep incline is to make certain you have three of your limbs firmly anchored with hand and footholds before moving the fourth. Always test footing and handholds before placing your weight on them. You'll discover that it is often rather easy to pull yourself up rifts in cliff or steep rock piles, but nearly impossible to descend safely without the security of a climbing rope. Don't climb under these conditions.

Talus slopes, composed of large stones or boulders, are located on mountainsides below steep cliffs. Proceed across them with caution, maintaining balance and testing each boulder for stability before stepping up on it. A walking staff is a big help negotiating this kind of country.

A *scree* slope composed of small stones requires a more aggressive approach. Take small steps, but keep moving steadily or you may find yourself slipping down the mountainside. Many hikers run down and across scree; this practice should be discouraged, for not only can it lead to a spill, but it damages the scree and makes it more difficult for others who use the trail to follow.

While climbing switchbacks, keep a lookout for rocks dislodged by hikers who may be above you. If you hear a shout of "Below!" or "Rock!,"

Talus slopes are notoriously unstable. Test the footing before putting your weight down.

Fear of Falling

Many otherwise brave human beings become dizzy or nauseous at extreme heights and when standing near drop-offs. People who are susceptible to the spinning sensation of vertigo cannot be trusted to maintain balance, while others simply become overwhelmed by fear and freeze up; they experience the "grip," to use rock climbing lingo. If a member of your party is afraid of heights or susceptible to vertigo, inquire about the trail before hiking. And if you find yourself in a situation where a companion freezes while traversing a ledge or otherwise treacherous terrain, tell them to look only at their boots, not into the space beyond, and talk them across in a calm voice. Extend a walking stick or rope, but assess your companion's condition carefully before extending your hand. He might panic and grapple with you, causing both of you to fall.

resist the temptation to look up. Crouch down and cover your head until the danger has passed. If you dislodge a rock, warn those below you by shouting as loudly as you can.

FORDING STREAMS

One of the benefits of using a topographical map is knowing in advance where stream crossings are and preparing accordingly.

Small creeks offer little obstacle to fit hikers. Just pick a narrow place and step across. But be careful. Trying to hop too far can result in a wet boot or sprained ankle. Better to walk up and down the bank as far as necessary to locate a natural bottleneck.

Wider streams are often bridged at trail crossings by logs or stepping stones. Worn smooth by water and the boots of countless hikers, they can be extremely slippery. A walking stick or hiking pole is an invaluable aid for keeping your balance. If you don't have one, look for a stout stick. Other hikes will have had the same idea, so often you'll find a suitable staff at the water's edge.

Sooner or later—sooner, if you hike in late spring or early summer when water levels are high—you'll come to a stream that can't be crossed without getting your feet wet. If it has a fine stone or sandy bottom, it's no problem to roll up your pant legs, hang your boots over your neck by their laces and pick your way across. Usually the safest crossings are at the shallow tailouts of big pools, where the stream is widest. Cross by walking up and across stream or, if circumstances don't permit that, down and across stream. Avoid crossing at right angles to the current, where water pressure is greatest. It's generally safer to hold hands with a partner than to cross alone. A larger party can cross as a "train," with each person placing his hands on the shoulder tops of the one in front. Always keep weaker hikers in the middle during crossings.

When I went on a extended cross-country skiing trip in Montana's Bob Marshall Wilderness a few years ago, we packed large plastic trash bags to use

On river crossings, use a walking staff or a stout stick as a third leg for better balance.

as makeshift hip boots for crossing the frigid water of the South Fork of the Flathead River. We took off our boots, slipped a bag over each leg and pulled on tennis shoes to cross. We stayed as dry as the old elk bones that littered the bank. Just make sure when using trash bags to slip some kind of overshoe over the plastic; left unprotected, the bag will tear from the abrasion of the stream bottom long before you reach the bank.

BUSHWHACKING

A trail is a buffer that holds the heart of wilderness at bay. It is like a road. You can sightsee from that road, and you can feel the breath of the country and listen to its song far more clearly than is possible from a car, but you will never know the secrets of dark forests or discover the hidden crannies in the mountains until you work up the courage to leave the path.

Bushwhacking, or cutting cross-country where no manmade trails exist, opens that door to discovery. But it also opens doors to uncertainty and apprehension. Without a line on a map to follow, you will no longer know exactly where you are. You will have to be a little more careful where you place your feet and you will come up against many natural obstacles, such as windfalls, boulder fields, or patches of brush that make the going difficult. At times, you'll have to detour from the direction you had intended to travel. You'll be forced into making decisions about which way to turn and unlike trail travel, you'll have to remember where you came from.

There are places where bushwhacking is not recommended. Fragile areas, including many canyon and alpine environments, can be easily damaged by cross-country travel. In muskeg and tundra, disturbed vegetation may take

Wading Tips

- Shuffle your feet during river crossings. If you step down heavily, it's easy to drive an unseen stick or sharp rock into your foot.

- You're always taking a chance of injury when wading barefoot. If you anticipate a stream crossing, pack along a pair of sandals or athletic shoes. Rubber overshoes that businessmen use to stretch over dress shoes are another option and weigh next to nothing.

- In mountainous country, it's usually safest to cross a stream early in the morning, when the water level is low. After the sun starts to melt the snow in the high country, the watercourse will not only be fuller, but murkier, which adds to the danger.

- On deep water crossings, undo your waist belt and chest strap before wading. In the event of a fall, you can slip your arms out of the shoulder straps and swim to safety much more easily than you can if buckled to the pack.

years to recover. National parks such as Yellowstone and Glacier also discourage off-trail travel because of the greater likelihood of encountering grizzly bears. Just as menacing are the three-lobed leaves of poison oak and poison ivy which render some New England low country and thousands of square miles of the California coast unappetizing for the wandering spirit.

But in temperate regions where forest floors are deep in decaying leaves or pine needles and the only trails are those left by the hooves of moose, deer and elk, bushwhacking does little damage to the environment. Each fall, I hike a hundred miles or more in the great robes of forest that cloak Montana mountainsides, looking for an elk to fill my freezer. Unless there is a snow cover, I almost never find any trace left by human beings.

The truth is that most hikers stick to the security of trails because they don't know how to use navigational aids and are petrified of becoming lost. But remember: Knowledge is courage. By learning how to find your way through wild country with or without a map and compass and how to survive an unexpected night outdoors, you'll gain the confidence to wander where your curiosity leads you.

CHAPTER
4

Staying Found, Surviving Being Lost

". . . he finally said, 'I guess you don't know much anyway, do you?' The boy (barefoot) answered, 'No, but I'm not lost.'

You may be the big toad in the puddle when you are at home but don't try to poke fun at the 'Small Town' folk until you are sure you are 'out of the woods.' "

LEON L. BEAN,
WRITING THE STORY OF A CITY HUNTER
LOST IN THE BIG MAINE WOODS

STAYING FOUND

The three basic questions of navigation—*Where am I? Where am I going? How do I get there?*—can usually be answered by hikers who have mastered two primitive methods of navigation. They are the "home base" system, which relies on the memorization of landmarks, so that a hiker orients himself by recognizing familiar trees, rocks, or other features of the country, and "dead reckoning," by which one calculates position by estimating the time and distance he has traveled from a previous point, as well as by the position of the sun and stars.

You may ask why someone who has a compass in his pocket or a GPS unit in his backpack should learn primitive methods of navigation. One reason is that modern aids can become lost or fail due to broken components or expired batteries. Another, more important reason is that people who rely exclusively upon magnetic needles and digital displays lose connection to the land under their feet. They may not become lost, but upon emerging from the woods they will not have earned the knowledge of the country that someone who has kept track of his position by memorizing landmarks, counting steps and thinking on his feet will have.

Orienting Position with Baselines

The key to staying found begins with baselines. A baseline can be a road, a powerline cut, a river, or a ridge line. Establish these lines with reference to your position before leaving the trailhead. They will serve as your

"Two roads diverged in the wood," Robert Frost wrote, "and I, I took the one less traveled by." If you choose less-traveled paths in heavy forest, pay attention to prominent landmarks such as this rock, so that you will recognize them when hiking out. To paraphrase Frost, it will make all the difference.

sun and stars to fix location and provide direction during the course of your hike. As you begin to walk, make a mental map as the country unfolds, memorizing or recording in a notebook as many details of the landscape as possible. Turn around every couple hundred feet. Rocks or trees marked for memory will look quite different when viewed from the other side. If you have to backtrack later on, this is the face of the mental map you'll have to rely upon. Estimate distance by keeping track of time, and, whenever you have an opportunity, climb a tree or walk to higher ground to note your location relative to the baselines.

Learn How to Walk a Straight Line

Being able to travel in a straight line is of vital importance to any hiker who bushwhacks into unfamiliar country.

Consider the following scenario: From the vantage of a ridge, you have a good view of the country and know which direction to walk to reach the road where you parked your car. But heavy forest lies in-between, and, as soon as you leave the high ground, the road will be out of sight until you actually step foot onto it.

Don't assume that you can walk straight to the road. For one thing, your legs are not exactly the same length. Your stride will always be shorter on one side. Given enough distance, you'll eventually turn in a circle—a feat I have accomplished in three different states! You also will have a natural tendency to follow the paths of least resistance and veer off course to avoid swamps, brushy areas or other natural barriers.

The only way to ensure walking a straight line is to align two objects, such as trees or rocks, along the your intended direction of travel (see below). Before reaching the first tree, line up a third one behind the second. By constantly keeping at least two objects in sight along your route, you'll be able to negotiate the forest on a fairly tight string.

When hiking, you have a natural tendency to drift off course. To walk a straight line, keep two objects lined up along your course in the distance. Before reaching the first, line up a third one.

Another challenge of hiking without a compass is knowing which way to turn once you reach the ridgeline where your tent is pitched, or which way to turn on the road to find your car. That's why it's wise to steer a course that takes you to one side of your destination, rather than trying to hit the mark straight on (see below).

A more difficult situation faces you when you hiked out from a dead-end road. If you head straight out from the car the chance of finding the vehicle upon your return, unless you've made an exact mental map for backtracking, is

When returning from a hike, plot a course that will take you to one side of your camp or car, rather than attempting to hit it straight on. That way, when you reach the road or river, you will have no doubt about which direction to turn.

fairly remote. In this situation, it's better to hike in a fairly straight line and keep track of the time that has elapsed before you turn around to head back. Then, walking by your watch, set a return course that will take a little to one side of the road. Continue hiking until you are certain you are past the road end. Then cut over to the road and hike back up it to the car (see below).

That's about all there is to staying found. You keep track of where you are going by referencing baselines and prominent land features, as well as by memorizing details along the trail. You keep track of where you are going by estimating how long you have traveled in a certain direction.

It is difficult to backtrack exactly to find a car at the end of a dead-end road. Return instead by walking to one side until you are certain you are past the dead end, then cut over to the road and walk back up.

Heavenly Help

If you become disoriented and can no longer locate points of reference, it may be time to look to the sky for help. As long as you know what direction you need to travel to reach a road or river that will lead you home, you can orient your internal compass by the sun and stars.

Two simple methods of fixing points of a compass are illustrated below.

To find directions in daylight, drive a stick into the ground and mark the end of its shadow with a stone. Wait 20 minutes and mark the end of the shadow with another stone. A line drawn from the first stone through the second will point east. This method works best near midday.

To find directions at night, face the North Star and drive a stick into the ground. Back up 20 feet and drive in a second stick, lining up the two sticks to point toward the North Star. A line drawn between the sticks will point north and south.
*(**Note:** To find Polaris, the North Star, locate the pointer stars on the bucket of Ursa Major, the Big Dipper. Calculate the space between those stars, then follow their direction five equal spaces to the North Star.)*

Estimating Distance

On level ground, walking at a steady pace, you can estimate relative distances by consulting your watch. Most hikers, unburdened by heavy packs, will walk from 2½ to 3½ miles per hour. Counting steps is more accurate, though it can become confusing when covering longer distances. One trick is to put a handful of pebbles into your right pocket. After each 100 steps, transfer one pebble to your left pocket. For a man of average height, or a fairly tall woman, each step on level ground covers about three feet, so 100 steps equals 100 yards.

You can map your progress on a piece of paper this way, and by fine-tuning the formula to match the exact length of your stride, estimate distances of a mile or so with fair accuracy.

> ### Folklore Guideposts: Fact or Fiction?
>
> Tree rings are narrowest on the north side, right? Well, sometimes. Folklore guideposts are just that, folklore: a combination of most-of-the-time truths and wishful thinking. Prevailing winds don't always blow from the same direction. And while it may be generally the case that moss grows on the north side of tree trunks, that the tops of trees point the rising sun and that conifers are bushiest on the side that faces south, local aberrations give many false readings. Look into the sky for your directions. The sun and stars always tell the truth.

The Magic Needle

Unquestionably, the compass is the cheapest and most reliable navigational tool available to hikers. Next to a calm, clear-thinking mind, it's the best insurance anyone has against getting lost.

A fixed-dial compasses may consist of nothing more than a needle and a face marked into eight quadrants: N, NE, E, SE, S, SW, W, and NW. I carry a simple bubble model that pins to a shirt. By periodically glancing at it, I can update my position with respect to baselines and prominent landmarks throughout the day and *stay found,* as opposed to resorting to a compass only after I become disoriented, which is a recipe for *getting lost.*

Keeping on a straight course is much easier when you refer to a compass. It is still necessary to align a sequence of objects along your line of travel, however, because you won't always be looking down at the compass and your legs will tend to move you off course one way or another.

To avoid lateral or sideways drift when progress is interrupted by a natural obstruction such as a lake, pick out a tall tree or other object on the far side that is along the intended direction of travel. When you reach it, take a new compass reading before continuing forward.

A fixed-dial compass has two limitations: it cannot be adjusted for declination, which is the difference in degrees between True North and magnetic North, and it cannot be used to plot a course on a topographic map. For those reasons, serious hikers also should carry a protractor-type compass, which has a rotating face marked off in 360 degrees and is mounted on a transparent baseplate.

To take a direct bearing on a landmark with a protractor compass, hold it in front of you at eye level. Most compasses have a sighting system that makes it easy to align the direction-of-travel arrow with your target. Then, holding the compass absolutely still, turn the compass housing until the magnetic needle lies directly over the orienting arrow (see illustration on facing page). Read your bearing in degrees at the base of the direction-of-travel arrow. At the same time, take a back bearing, which is the opposite of your direct bearing—your back bearing is your forward bearing minus 180 degrees.

By taking a back bearing, you don't have to be so meticulous about lateral drift as you hike. If you stray a little bit to one side, you will still be walking toward your direct bearing, but your back bearing will change. When that happens, shift to one side or the other until you come back in line. This occurs when the compass realigns to read both your original direct bearing and original back bearing.

Reading Maps

Topographical maps are essentially overhead drawings of sections of land. Forested country is shaded green; open valleys and hillsides are left white. Differences in elevation are marked by contour lines. Typically, every fifth line is darker and somewhere along its length the elevation is marked. Lines that are closely spaced indicate a steep slope, whereas those spaced far apart indicate flat or gently rolling country. The contour lines assume a V shape where they follow watercourses, which are marked by blue lines. The V points uphill. Ridges that slope from a mountain peak are also marked by V lines, the V pointing downhill. U-shaped lines indicate relatively broad river valleys or gentle hills. A pattern like the whorl of a fingerprint indicates land rising toward a peak (see illustration on page 58).

With a little practice, you will be able to pick up a topographic map and read it in relief, visualizing the rise and fall of the landforms that separate different watercourses. Remember, however, that distances marked on the map do not account for changes in elevation; in mountainous country, they will seem much greater. You also will have a tendency to overestimate how far you have traveled.

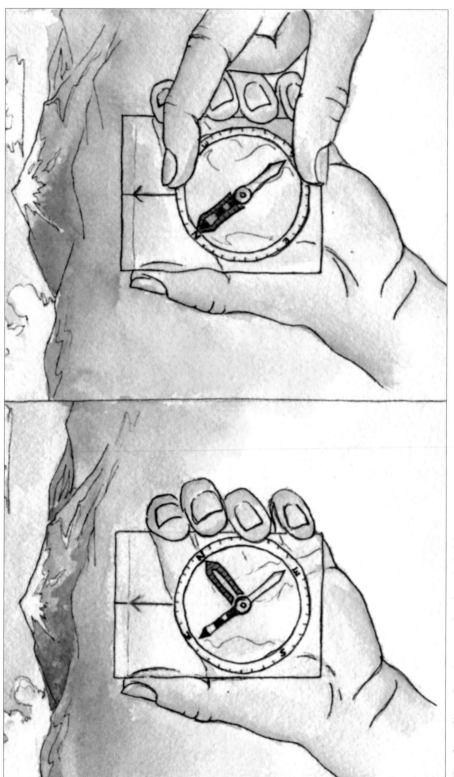

To take a direct bearing on a landmark, hold your compass at eye level with the direction-of-travel arrow pointed at your target. Holding the compass still, turn the housing until the magnetic arrow lies within the lines of the orienting arrow. Read the bearing in degrees at the base of the direction-of-travel arrow.

Three views of a mountain: on the bottom, as it appears to the eye; at middle, superimposed by contour lines representing elevation changes; on top, as it is represented on a topographic map. Once you gain experience interpreting contour lines and symbols, you will be able to read a map in relief and visualize the country you will be traversing.

The most useful maps for map and compass navigation are the U.S. Geological Survey (USGS) 7.5-minute series, which cover an area of roughly 6 by 8 miles. There also are 15-minute maps available for some areas (these maps are slowly being phased out in favor of the 7.5 series), which offer a little less

A good topographic map is an indispensable tool for wilderness navigation.

detail but cover more country, a plus for long hikes that take you across several quadrants. USGS maps are widely available in outdoor stores and can usually be obtained locally if you're on vacation. However, maps of popular backcountry areas often sell out. If you know where you'll be hiking, you can mail-order them through the Earth Science Information Center by phoning (800) USA-MAPS. They can provide you with an index of maps covering the state, so you'll know which ones to order.

Map and Compass Navigation

The fly in the ointment when you navigate by map is declination. All U.S. Geological Survey maps are based on geographic or true north, whereas your compass reads magnetic north. The difference, or angle of declination, is marked at the base of every map. In the lower 48 states, the discrepancy is never more than 25 degrees one way or other.

The simplest way to compensate is to buy a compass that adjusts for declination by turning a dial. Some protractor compasses do not have this feature, so be sure to check.

Once you've adjusted your compass, you're ready to plot a course (see illustration below). By penciling each leg of your hike on the map with the corresponding bearings, you not only know exactly where you are going, but if you need to backtrack later on, you can do so by following back bearings to the point of origin.

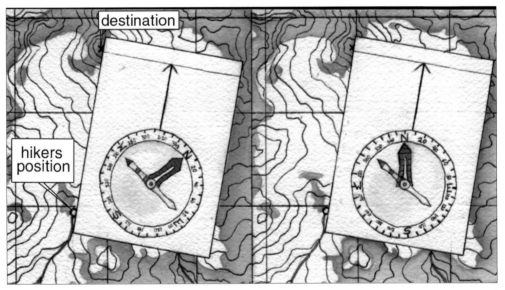

1. To plot a course, use a straight edge to draw a line between your position on the map and the destination of your hike. Extend it far enough to bisect a line of longitude or the vertical border of the map.   2. Align one of the long edges of the compass baseplate with the line you have penciled.   3. Turn the dial on the compass until the N and S on the face align with one of the vertical lines on the map.   4. Ignore the magnetic needle. Read the course you want to travel at the base of the direction-of-travel arrow.   5. Now fold the map. Holding your compass in front of you, turn your body until the magnetic needle lies directly over the outline of the orienting arrow.   6. Follow the direction-of-travel arrow toward your destination.

A hiker who has neglected his compass and become unsure of his location can fix his position on the map as long as he is able to see two prominent landmarks that also are marked on the map (see illustration).

To determine your position on a map, find two landmarks that intercept your location at about a 90-degree angle. Use your outstretched arms to estimate the angle. Take a back bearing for each of the landmarks. Mark them on the map using the same method for taking a forward bearing. The only difference is that when you rotate the compass case, align the south end of the magnetic needle over the orienting arrow. When you draw the backbearing lines, they will intersect the map at your location.

As with any skill, the best way to learn navigating by map and compass is through personal instruction. Courses are periodically offered through local outdoor societies and adult education programs. The U.S. Orienteering Federation, P.O. Box 1444, Forest Park, GA 30298, telephone (404) 363–2110, can put you in touch with a program in your area.

Altimeters: The Climber's Companion

An altimeter measures elevation through changes in atmospheric pressure. Altimeters are about the size and weight of an old-fashioned pocket watch, with a dial face marked off in 20-foot increments and a needle that indicates elevation. You can buy digital altimeters, but they are more prone to failure.

In some ways, an altimeter is more useful than a compass if you hike in the mountains. For example, it greatly increases your chances of finding a secluded campsite in country where visibility is limited. Just make sure to jot down the camp elevation before leaving on a dayhike, then return on a contour that will intersect the camp.

Keep in mind that altimeters are subject to changes in the weather. Reset the dial whenever you come to a saddle, mountain peak, pond, or other feature that has its elevation marked on the map, in order to keep errors to a minimum.

Global Positioning System (GPS)—Too Good to Be True?

If staying found is knowing approximately where you are at all times, then getting lost with GPS technology is just about impossible. With a tap of your fingertip on a receiver the size of a small cell phone, satellite triangulation renders your position to the screen in longitude and latitude. If you have stored the location of your car or campsite in the system's memory, another finger tap will give you its bearing and the distance you must travel to find it. A backtracking feature can retrace your steps to each waypoint locked in during your travel.

Is GPS the greatest navigational aid since the compass? Or is it a formula for disaster?

I think most experienced hikers would say it can be both. For finding campsites hidden away in heavy forest or for intricate point-to-point navigation, GPS technology is unsurpassed. But GPS also can serve as a crutch that takes the place of woodsmanship. It can act as a security blanket that encourages inexperienced hikers to wander farther than they should in country where they shouldn't. And, of course, GPS units are subject to mechanical and battery failure.

If you decide to buy a GPS, be aware that much of gadgetry on more expensive models is unnecessary. Maps built into the receiver are of no use for land navigation. Designer icons, temperature sensors, and color displays only clutter up the screen. As one friend of mine puts it, "If you want entertainment, get a Game Boy."

What you should look for is a 12-channel parallel receiver that has plot, status, navigation, and position screens and is capable of storing several hundred waypoints in its memory bank. Buy extra batteries and carry them in your pack. I've found the manuals that come with some GPS units to be unnecessarily complicated. You can order a good instructional video that will work with any unit from GPS Outfitters, Dept. FS, 9416 Knox Dr., Overland Park, KS 66212, phone (800) 447–4868.

My advice for anyone considering GPS is to become proficient with map and compass first. That is the foundation for all serious navigation.

SURVIVING BEING LOST

Sooner or later nearly everyone who hikes in wild country becomes lost, or at least a little turned around. If this happens and you cannot rely on a compass or other navigational aid for help, the most important thing to remember is that your enemy is not the impending night or a falling barometer. It's your own panic.

First, sit down. Eat a bite of sandwich or a granola bar. It will help you calm your nerves. Take a strip of toilet paper or orange marking ribbon and tie it to a tree. From now on, consider this spot to be **home base.**

Think back. When was the last time you were certain of your surroundings? Can you retrace your steps to that place? Put your pack on and try to find it, marking your passage as you go. The easiest way to do this is by tearing two-inch pieces of orange marking ribbon and affixing them to tree branches at regular intervals. Toilet paper also works. If you don't have any, bend back the tops of bushes or small trees as you hike. The pale undersides of the leaves will mark your return trail.

If you don't recognize any familiar place, return to home base. After you've rested up a while, begin exploring the country by making short, straight-line excursions, once again taking your pack and marking your progress. Climb a tree or walk to higher ground to get a better vantage point. Return to home base after each excursion. If extended reconnaissance in several directions doesn't reveal any familiar landmarks or baselines, review your options. Search and rescue leaders stress that most hikers are not too far out of their way when they first feel "lost." In fact, quite often they are in familiar country, but either fog has reduced visibility or snow or unusual lighting has transformed its appearance. If you had the forethought to leave a message at home detailing your whereabouts, then searchers will come looking for you. The farther you travel from home base, the longer it's going to take them to track you down.

If it's growing dark, or if a storm is brewing, it would be foolhardy to hike any farther. Build a shelter from your survival gear or from materials at hand, gather some wood in case you need a fire, and wait until morning.

If you decide to try to find your way out, make a plan. I once found myself lost in a cedar forest in northern Michigan. Twice I turned a circle and came back onto my own track in the mud. The second time it happened I felt a flush of fear and nearly panicked, although the area I was hiking in was bound on one side by the Manistee River and two other sides by roads, and at no point during my hike could I have been more than half a mile from one of them. Finally, I decided to walk in a grid pattern, counting my steps and making each leg of the grid longer than the last (see illustration). I came within sound of the river in 15 minutes.

Walking in a regular pattern is more difficult and time consuming in mountainous country. There, your chances are generally better by following the flow of water. Small creeks will hook up with larger streams and eventually reach a road. However, be aware that some streams meander through bogs, plum-

If you get lost in flat country, walk a right-angle grid pattern to intercept a road, creek or other known baseline. Make each leg of the grid twice as long as the last, estimating distance by your watch or by counting steps.

met over impassable cliffs, or rocket through box canyons where deadfall, sheer rock faces, and jumbled boulders make travel hazardous. Often, it is quicker and safer to get up on a ridge to one side of a watercourse and follow it to lower elevation.

Look also for well-worn game trails or cattle tracks. They usually follow easy contours and eventually lead to water.

Always make time to mark your trail. This not only allows you the option of returning to home base—something you should seriously consider if a long day of walking doesn't improve your situation—it also gives searchers a way to track you down.

Building Shelter

Each year, our newspaper reports the tragic deaths of people who succumb to hypothermia in the mountains near my home. Some of the victims are hunters and cross-country skiers who are unprepared for the weather, but the casualties also include climbers and hikers who freeze to death in the summer, in temperatures that never dropped below freezing.

In nearly all cases, the victims had panicked and soaked their clothes with sweat. When too tired to go any farther, the combination of wet clothing and wind chill led to hypothermia. Recognize this urge to panic for what it is—a message for you to stop blindly walking and stay put. Had the hikers who perished used their energy to construct shelters and build fires before darkness fell, rather than walk blindly into the night, many would be alive today.

Building shelter creates the impression of a camp, which can be of great psychological value to someone who feels lost. The best lightweight shelter a hiker can carry is a tarp, 6 or 8-feet square, made of coated nylon or clear plastic Visqueen, which is sold by the foot in hardware stores. (For instructions on making tarps and ways to rig them as emergency shelters, see Chapter 6).

If you don't have a tarp, keep in mind that a shelter can be as simple as a recess under an overhanging ledge, a hollow chopped into the massed branches of a big downfall or a grove of trees out of the wind. One of the best natural shelters, available coast to coast in northern latitudes, is a bushy spruce tree with limbs draping to the ground. Saw or break enough branches on the lee side to sit with your back against the trunk and close off the opening with the branches.

Inuit have survived temperatures of 50 degrees below zero simply by squatting down with their backs to the wind, so that their skin parkas draped to the snow over their knees, creating a pocket of still air. You can cocoon inside an emergency space blanket to the same effect. One 12-year-old boy in Montana survived three nights of zero weather wearing only cotton pants, a sweatshirt, and a hunting vest. He put the vest on backward to get more insulation against his chest, stuck his hands up under his sleeves, and curled under the lee of a rock ledge to get out of the wind. The searchers who found him called his survival a miracle, but there would be many other miracles if lost hikers put their faith in shelter rather than their legs.

Fire

Second to shelter is the survival value of fire. Besides creating warmth, one of its most important benefits is drying clothes. Nothing hastens the onset of hypothermia more quickly than damp clothing, which is why serious hikers should invest in underwear that wicks perspiration away from the body and outer clothes that allow moisture to evaporate and provide insulation even when partially wet.

Fire can serve as a distress signal, a means of melting snow to drink and a way to cook food. It soothes nerves, builds confidence, and encourages the lost or injured to stay in one place.

Always pack windproof, waterproof matches, and tuck into your survival kit some kind of alternative fire-starting devices as well, such as a butane lighter and flint and steel.

Something to provide a steady flame is needed. A tube of fire-starting paste works, as does a candle stub. For years I carried a 10-minute highway flare, sealed in a plastic bag to keep it dry. Once, when I became sick while hiking alone on a cold day in the mountains, my hands shook so badly that I had difficulty collecting tinder. In desperation, I heaped a pile of dead branches together with my boots and struck the flare. Up until the moment the flames caught, I had wondered if the half-pound of extra weight was worth packing. It was.

Tinder is the foundation of any fire. Good sources include grass, moss, pine needles, and bark. In much of the Northeast, birch is a common woodland tree, especially in river valleys. In an emergency, you can tear a strip of bark off either a living or fallen tree and remove fine strips from the inner layer. It is resinous and burns with a strong flame even when wet. Don't overlook the contents of your pockets and pack; lint, hat linings, plastic badges, notebook paper, even dollar bills will burn. Thread unraveled from synthetic clothing will burn. Shaved hair will burn.

After collecting tinder and rolling it into a loose ball, collect as many tiny twigs as you can find. The undersides of conifers are usually densely quilled with dry twigs and have possibly saved more lives of wilderness wanderers than the compass. Make a pile of the twigs and another pile composed of small, broken tree branches. Make longer excursions from home base to drag in larger logs. In pine woods, pitch stumps can usually be unearthed by kicking and pulling at them. They smoke like hell, but are saturated with resin and burn much longer than logs.

If the ground is wet, start your fire on top of the dry undersides of a log or a large piece of bark. Create a windbreak with your pack or anything else at hand. Build a teepee fire, leaning tiny twigs over the tinder, then pencil-diameter pieces of stick over the tinder. Keep your teepee loose to permit air circulation. Once the flames are licking, add more pencil-sized wood. Gradually build up the fire with larger sticks and finally sections of log. If the purpose of your fire is to provide a cheery light and sense of security, keep it small. But if the ground is wet or the night cold, build it up. A small fire will sap its strength just trying to dry out the ground.

You can't buy a cheaper insurance policy for wilderness survival than waterproof, windproof matches and a cube of paraffin to sustain the flame. Hone your fire-building skills in wet, snowy, and windy conditions, so you will have gained experience and confidence before an emergency arises.

Before turning in for the night, drag in as much big wood as you think is necessary for an all-night fire. Then go back out and drag in another load the same size. Let the fire burn down to a deep bed of glowing embers and place a couple green logs on top. If laid parallel to each other, the flames will lick up between them and burn for many hours.

Then relax as best you can. Sit on your pack or a square of closed-cell pad if you brought one. Spread your poncho or rain clothes underneath your body. Don't count on a good night's sleep—you aren't going to get one.

If you grow cold, stand up and walk around. Windmill your arms to promote circulation in your upper body. Then sit or lie back down for snatches of sleep.

Today's search and rescue squads, aided by aerial reconnaissance and tracking dogs, act so quickly and cover ground so efficiently that few hikers who stay put after becoming lost are forced to spend a second night in the open.

That doesn't mean that improving your shelter, building signal fires or SOS signs out of logs in a clearing, and looking for food and water should not be on your agenda for the morning. They should be. But the key to survival is using your head to get through the first night. It is the one survival tool you can't do without.

To these sound suggestions, I will add one more. Many children have been taught to respect private property. One small Montana boy who was lost spent three nights in the open, even though he had seen a ranch house in the distance. Assure kids that it's okay to cross fences and ignore "No Trespassing" signs when they become lost, and that no one will be mad if they knock on a stranger's door.

When Children Become Lost

The Hug-A-Tree Program lists eight guidelines for ensuring children's safety if they become separated from adults while hiking:

1. At home, have your child walk across a piece of aluminum foil with the shoes he or she will hike in. Searchers can use the impression to identify tracks.

2. Give each child a large plastic trash bag to use as a poncho to shelter from the elements and a shrill whistle to signal for help.

3. Keep children oriented during hiking. Point out prominent landmarks and baselines, as well as the position of the sun and what it means.

4. Assure kids that you won't be mad should they become separated from you. Some children have ignored the calls of searchers because they were afraid they would be in trouble for getting lost.

5. Tell your children that many people will come looking for them, so they should stay put rather than attempt to find their way back to the car.

6. Instruct them to pick a big tree by the side of the trail (unless there is a thunderstorm) and wait there. The tree or other landmark grounds them, helps them avoid panic, and keeps them in one place.

7. Assure children that wild animals will not attack them. If they hear a noise, whether in the day or night, they are to shout at it and blow the whistle. If it's an animal, it will run away. If it's a person, they will be found.

8. Have children wear bright clothing and tell them to get in an open area near their tree and make themselves appear big for aerial rescue. Tell them to wave their clothing or packs should they hear an airplane.

SECTION
II

BACKPACKING

ikers make the natural transition to backpacking for many reasons. Most share a common ground with dayhiking—the impulse to explore, to walk among the glories of nature and to develop self-reliance while strengthening bonds with our companions. Yet there are rewards from actually living in wild country that cannot be realized through dayhiking, even if our walks take us many miles from the paved filaments of civilization.

When you know you will be returning home before darkness, a corner of your mind tends to remain behind. Because you do not feel your heart quicken when the wall of tree trunks grows solid in the twilight, when the murmur of the creek grows more insistent, it is easier to maintain a distance from the country, to stay more of a sightseer. That attitude changes when you know that the forest will serve as your bedroom. By living and sleeping outside, with only a minimum of gear to insulate you from nature's mercurial moods, you become much more of a participant in the pulse of its life.

This transformation doesn't happen overnight. Most of us cannot walk away from a daily existence that is defined by obligations to work and family, and that is bound by perimeters of steel and concrete, then pick up a trail through the forest, lie down on the earth and expect to sleep soundly. Backpacking requires fundamental

Backpacking is a journey, not a destination. Its rewards can be reaped along the trail, as well as at the day's end.

Beyond this portal lies wilderness. It is a backpacker's nirvana, but to truly feel at home in remote country one must invest time; the ability to relax into the rhythms and profound silences of nature won't occur overnight.

adjustments in the rhythms of our lives. The pack takes some getting used to. Straps chaff and untested muscles become sore. When you are out of the routine, setting up camp, purifying water and cooking dinner can be a bumpy process, especially if you're exhausted and wait until evening to stop hiking, as is so often the case the first day on the trail. And a three-quarter inch pad seems like precious little cushioning when you are accustomed to a mattress.

But the largest adjustment is mental. My friend Joe Gutkoski, who probably spends more time backpacking alone each year than most of us do in our lifetimes, still finds that he is not immediately acclimated upon his returns to the wilderness. He says that for the first couple days, he looks for excuses to turn toward home. After the second night, though, he says, "I don't care if I ever go back."

Perhaps epiphany is too strong a word to describe his awakening on that third morning. In my own experience, it is more like a subtle reversal of perspective, a matter of looking forward down the trail, rather than gauging the distance back to the road. The vestiges of urban longing have been shed like an old skin. My muscles and skeletal frame have adjusted to the weight of the pack, leaving me free to drink in the sights and odors along the trail. And now that I am dependent on the natural world to provide me with water, with a flat place to rest my head, with shelter from a storm, it has become a partner in the journey. I have become a strand of the Earth's web, of the intricate flux of energy that underlies its surface beauty and supports the tapestry of all life.

For many people, this process of immersion or relaxation *into* nature is the richest reward of backpacking. The fact that you must commit time and energy to realize that goal only makes its attainment more special.

CHAPTER 5

Planning a Backpacking Trip

"All paths lead nowhere, so it is important to choose a path that has heart."

Carlos Castaneda

Most of us equate backpacking with wilderness—rugged mountain ranges or arid canyons winding miles from the nearest road. The prospect of venturing that far the first time out can be intimidating for newcomers who question whether they are in shape to endure a long trip with a heavy pack, or if they have the skills to navigate through remote country. Money and travel concerns may also hold people back.

The fact is that your first backpacking trip can be inexpensive, short in duration, and undertaken with a light load. And chances are that no matter where you live, backpacking opportunities exist close to home.

For example, New Yorkers can drive away from the congestion of Manhattan and in less than two hours park at a trailhead in either Harriman State Park or Catskill Mountain State Park, both of which offer hundreds of miles of well-marked trails. If that's too far away, the Appalachian Trail runs within 70 miles of the city. Turn south and you can walk all the way to Georgia; a few hundred miles north and east the trail ends atop Mt. Katahdin.

Utopia for a backpacker may be the view of a sunlit butte from a remote campground, but for your first trip, don't overlook the many opportunities close to home.

INFORMATION SOURCES

The Internet

The Internet has opened up a wealth of information to prospective backpackers that previously could have been obtained only through exhaustive research and long-distance phone calls. Some of the more comprehensive Web sites currently available are listed in the Reference section of this book. A keyword search for a specific park, refuge, or national forest will nearly always turn up useful information. Also keep in mind that many periodicals, including the immensely informative magazine, *Backpacker,* are available on-line with the click of a mouse.

Local Outfitters

Outfitting stores that specialize in hiking and backpacking gear are the best sources of information on local trails. Many outfitters also rent basic backpacking gear, so there's no need to invest in sleeping bags, tents, or other technical gear until you've put enough miles on your boots to make an educated decision about what suits you best.

Hiking Clubs

Local hiking clubs and chapters of national organizations such as the Audubon Society, National Wildlife Federation, the American Hiking Society, the Appalachian Mountain Club, and the Sierra Club are good sources of backpacking information. Look in the Reference section for addresses of national headquarters. A quick call will put you in touch with representatives in your area. Many clubs sponsor dayhikes and group backpacking trips; sometimes a calendar of upcoming trips will be posted on the bulletin boards of outfitting stores or in the activities section of your newspaper. Beginning backpackers may be relieved to have an experienced leader for their first trips; others who have trouble finding companions to hike with will appreciate the chance to forge new friendships along the trail. The cost of these trips is usually minimal or covered by membership fees, which clubs use to maintain trail systems.

Land Agencies

The National Forest Service and Bureau of Land Management (BLM) are caretakers of millions of acres of some of the best remaining wild country in our nation. Regional offices can provide maps and booklets on local opportunities for hikers and backpackers. Also check out national and state parks in your region, as well as National Wildlife Refuges and National Monuments. The Reference section of this book provides information on how to contact national land agencies, but you can often save yourself the cost of a long distance call by thumbing through the state and federal sections of your phone book for regional offices.

Books and Travel Guides

Some publishing houses, such as Countryman Press, Foghorn Press, and Falcon Press offer hiking, backpacking and camping guides for many states and regions. Some guides are general, overviewing major trail systems in a state or region. Others can be quite specific, providing topographical maps and detailed information on the hiking trails in an area. See the Reference section for a list of some of the most popular and helpful guidebook series.

HOW TO PLAN A BACKPACKING TRIP

Making Sense of Trails

Finding places to backpack is not difficult. The greater problem is negotiating the information overload to whittle down the choices, factoring in such variables as seasonal rains or snowmelt, breeding cycles of bothersome insects, and difficulty of terrain. Trails are not created equal. Some will be narrow, poorly marked, or obliterated in places by roads, or will simply disappear in rocky terrain, leaving you wondering which way to turn. Others may be well-marked, but permit multiple uses such as off-road vehicle travel that can put a damper on your enthusiasm.

Most trail systems in national and state parks are wide and clearly marked. These trails can be popular—so much so that in places like Yosemite and Grand Canyon National Parks, you must make reservations in advance, not just to backpack, but sometimes to dayhike as well. On the plus side, you will not be bothered by ATVs and your vistas will not be compromised by forest clearcuts. You'll seldom go more than a few miles without seeing other hikers, but many novice backpackers may be more than willing to give up some solitude for the comfort of a passing smile and the security of knowing other people will be nearby in case they need help.

Designated wilderness areas offer some of most pristine backpacking experiences. Major trails tend to be clearly marked and traffic can range from heavy (in areas near urban centers) to practically non-existent. I've had the privilege on several occasions of backpacking deep into Montana's Bob Marshall Wilderness, more than 30 miles from the nearest roads, where the feeling of isolation was so profound that I felt as if I been transported into country as yet unexplored by human beings. Some who have visited the Bob Marshall and other remote wildernesses become unnerved by their vast silences. For others, the primordial forests reconnect them with the Earth in a way that is unmatched by any other environment.

National forests and desert BLM lands can be on a par with wilderness with regard to unblemished horizons and untrammeled footpaths. In places, they offer an attractive alternative to hiking in the national parks that adjoin their borders. For example, the Stanislaus National Forest, just north of California's Yosemite National Park, mirrors Yosemite's much-heralded beauty, with dozens of alpine lakes nestling underneath rocky crags. The trail system is clearly marked and you do not have to apply months in advance for a permit to backpack. The same can be said for the national forest lands that surround Yellowstone National Park in Idaho, Montana, and Wyoming.

Something to keep in mind is that travel restrictions on forest and BLM lands vary widely. Maps obtained at regional offices are usually color-coded, indicating areas where off-road vehicle use is permitted, as well as trails that are open to foot and horse traffic only. But the

You may have better luck discovering solitude in remote backcountry beyond park borders. Wilderness depends more on the nature of the country than it does on the land agency that governs it. Some of the most pristine backpacking is on national forest lands that are adjacent to popular national parks.

small scale does not permit the detail that backpackers need, and older maps may not show logging and mining roads that have been recently constructed. Also, place names on maps and trailhead signs don't always match.

Call regional headquarters for up-to-date information on areas you are interested in visiting.

Maps

Because U.S. Geological Survey maps detail changes in topography and are indispensable for map and compass navigation, they are a fixture in the pockets of serious backpackers. However, individual USGS quadrangles don't cover a lot of country; hikers on flat ground may find themselves traversing two or three 7.5-minute quads in a single day.

If you are planning a trip into a wilderness area or National Park, look in outfitting stores for larger-format (15-minute) USGS maps that include several quads of the region. These maps give a better overview of the country, while still providing the detail necessary for map and compass work. Laminated maps hold up better in adverse weather.

Forest Service and BLM maps cover entire management districts, providing hikers with a comprehensive view that individual topographic maps can't match. Another plus is that updated editions may include information on trail restrictions and logging roads that are not marked on the USGS quads. These maps aren't marked in contour lines, but do designate road and trail

The Dolorme Atlas/Gazetteer series is a complete set of topographic maps for individual states. Map scale is small, but trails are marked and numbered, making them a useful alternative to the quadrangles on U.S. Geological Survey (USGS) maps.

numbers, which USGS quads do not. By carrying one of these maps in addition to topographic maps, you'll get a better sense of the country than you would by packing only one or the other.

Many guidebooks provide topographic maps with detailed trail descriptions. The maps may not include infor-

> ### Keep Your Maps Readable
>
> Maps don't hold up very well in rainy weather. You can weatherproof your USGS quadrant maps with spray-on lacquers or acrylics sold in artist supply stores. Some outfitting shops that specialize in hiking gear also sell sprays for weatherproofing.
>
> Fold maps inside heavy-duty reclosable plastic bags to protect them from the elements and keep them in the top pocket of your pack, where they are easy to access and won't be crushed by other gear.

mation on declination, and, due to space limitations, show very little country to either side of the trail. But they will be more than adequate for on-trail hiking. Hiking clubs also reproduce and update existing maps to detail stretches of the trails they maintain.

Map atlases like the *Delorme Atlas/Gazetteer* series provide topographic maps for many states. A lot of country is crammed onto each page and detail is given short shrift. But the maps do include road and trail numbers, and if you accept their limitations, they may be adequate for shorter trips. They will also be useful if you have a change of plans and find yourself off the map when using one of your regular topos. *Trails Illustrated* also offers an excellent series of topographical maps of popular mountain ranges and national parks, on a scale that is large enough for casual hiking and backpacking.

You can also purchase maps on CD-ROM. For example, a CD-ROM of Yellowstone National Park sold by Navitrak includes 60 USGS quadrangles for a total cost that runs less than $1 per map. If you have no need for that many maps of an area, keep in mind that some outfitters that subscribe to a CD-ROM program will print individual maps for you from one of their computers.

Look in the Reference section for information on ordering these and many other types of maps.

The Importance of Timing

In nature, there are seasons within seasons. For example, summer in my part of the Rocky Mountains technically begins in June, but on the night of the solstice many higher elevation trails will still be slumbering underneath a blanket of snow. Early July can provide excellent hiking: warm days, cool nights, and not too many mosquitoes. Or, it can rain every day. Late July is more reliable in terms of weather, but the insects are at their peak then and can make life miserable. By the second week in August, crisp nights are beginning to put a lid on insect activity and hiking conditions are perfect—unless it's been an exceptionally dry year, when forest fires become a concern.

Every region in our country has its own idiosyncrasies, so do your homework before planning a vacation.

Gradients and Mileage

Generally speaking, fit backpackers carrying moderate loads—a moderate load being about one-quarter of the hiker's body weight—can comfortably cover six to eight miles over gently rolling terrain in the course of a day. Twelve to 16 miles is nothing out of the ordinary for backpackers on long treks, such as the Pacific Crest Trail, but those distances are achieved only after a week or more of on-trail conditioning.

On level ground, backpackers walk at about the same pace as casual dayhikers. But climbing a steep incline is much tougher with 40 pounds on your back than it is when you carry little more than a water bottle. When planning your first trip, err on the conservative side. Four or five miles a day is plenty. Backpacking isn't a contest and you'll appreciate having a couple of hours for lazing around camp, fishing, or indulging your passion for wildflowers before it's time to cook supper and settle in for the night.

Probably the best introduction to backpacking is a two- or three-day circuit on a well-marked trail with a total of no more than a 1,000-foot change in elevation. Loop trails that start and end at the same point are both more interesting than up-and-back routes and psychologically less exhausting, because you remain focused on exploring

Backcountry Huts: The Hard-Sided Alternative

Our country does not have the well-developed system of backcountry huts that are common along many trail systems in Europe. Still, there are a number of places where you can reserve shelters in advance. This offers inexperienced hikers an entree into backpacking without the burden of having to carry a lot of weight. Huts also are a good choice for parents with small children.

Shelters along parts of the Appalachian Trail can be reserved through The Appalachian Mountain Club Huts; phone 1–603–466–2727. Vermont's Long Trail, running the length of the state, is studded with many shelters. Montana's Glacier Park offers hikers the opportunity of staying in two backcountry chalets that provide candlelight dinners with gorgeous mountain window dressing, as well as the chance to see native wildlife.

Check with the public land agencies in the region you want to backpack for hutting opportunities.

the new country up the trail, rather than on how far you'll have to backtrack to reach the road.

Estimating Time and Distance in Mountainous Terrain

Never calculate distance alone when planning a trip. Always factor in elevation gains. Novice backpackers should allow at least 40 minutes for each mile of trail, plus an additional hour for each 1,000 feet of elevation gain. Add 10 minutes for rest stops after every 50 minutes of hiking, and you can see that a four- or five-mile hike in the mountains can easily take up the better part of the day.

BACKPACKING WITH CHILDREN

Parents who take up backpacking are often in a position where it's difficult to leave children behind. Having successfully taken their kids dayhiking, they wonder if they are ready to backpack, or at what age they will be ready.

Most of the books I have referenced do not recommend backpacking with children who are under the ages of seven or eight. Having backpacked with my own children when they were five and seven years old, I reluctantly have to agree. While most parents would never be so negligent as to permit their children to wander out of sight and become lost, the mental strain of keeping a constant eye on children in camp and along the trail, while indulging their

Backpacking with children this young can be a rewarding, if trying, experience. Don't expect to get anywhere in a hurry and plan to spend more time in camp than on the trail.

natural tendency to dawdle or balk at walking farther when the going becomes difficult, can make the entire experience exasperating.

Another drawback is that four- and five-year-olds cannot be expected to carry their share of the load. Parents will have to assume the extra burden of toting sleeping bags and food in their own packs. (However, even young kids do need to carry whistles, ponchos, trail munchies, and water in their daypacks for safety reasons.)

If you decide to take youngsters backpacking, understand that the difficulty you may have experienced adjusting to your kids' slower pace on dayhikes will be compounded when you are burdened by a heavy pack. One way to make an end-run around this problem is for parents to switch off at being the watchdog, allowing one to hike a half-mile or so up the trail at his own pace, then wait. When the rest of the family catches up, it's the other parent's turn to be the leap-frog.

Don't expect to cover more than a couple miles in a day. The dictum that backpacking is a journey, not a destination, doesn't apply to parents with four-year-olds. Redefine your idea of backpacking to include much less trail time and much more time in camp. That's where the children will be happiest.

Eight-year-olds have usually developed enough endurance to hike several miles at a reasonable pace and will be strong enough to take a little of the burden off your back and place it on their own. But you shouldn't expect a child to tote 10 or 15 pounds of gear in the same daypacks he or she wears to school. Get your child a real backpack, with either an internal or external frame and a padded hip belt. L.L. Bean advertises children's size packs in their catalogs and chances are that your local outfitter will have a couple models from which to choose. Remember that kids' smaller bones don't need as much cushioning from the hard ground as ours do; an inexpensive closed-cell pad a half-inch in thickness will be plenty. And children don't sweat a great deal until puberty kicks in, which means they can often get away with everyday cotton clothing. Just make certain each child has a good fleece or wool jacket and a warm hat for chilly nights. Don't forget to pack extra tennis shoes or sandals for the kids to wear as a backup if their shoes get wet.

Look in the Reference section for suggested titles of books written about hiking and backpacking with children. You can learn some tricks from them, but your kids will teach you all you really need to know on the first few miles of the trail. Just remember that the key to *their* enjoyment is *your* patience. Cater to their curiosity by making frequent stops to examine bugs, snakes, or other wildlife, and don't place an emphasis on covering too many miles before making camp.

CHAPTER
6

The House on Your Back

"Most of the luxuries, and many of the so-called comforts of life, are not only indispensable, but positive hindrances to the elevation of mankind."
HENRY DAVID THOREAU

My first backpacking outfitter was the Salvation Army. A friend had invited me on a weekend climb to the top of Washington's Mount St. Helens. I had driven west from Ohio with nothing more than tennis shoes and the clothes on my back. Having little money for boots or proper clothing, I had to forgo a trip to the REI outfitter in Seattle, which was the Holy Grail for West Coast backpackers, for the thrift store in downtown Olympia.

A couple days later my friend and I stood at 9,677 feet on the lip of the St. Helens caldera—he wearing a Kelty backpack with its heliarc-welded aluminum frame, I straining under my Army surplus rucksack, with a tumpline across my forehead to take some of the weight off my back.

When the volcano erupted a couple years later in 1980, the earth where we left our bootprints became nothing but sky. The rucksack has disappeared into thin air as well, gone I don't know where—and thank the Lord, because a tumpline is no way to pack a heavy load. My head ached for days after that hike.

Backpacking gear today is light-years advanced from what it was then. Modern outfitters offer such a dizzying display of high-tech equipment that newcomers can become overwhelmed by the selections, not to mention intimidated by the price tags. The truth is that you can get in on the ground level of

A backpack is a ticket to freedom. With all the provisions needed for a week-long trip, these hikers are limited only by the strength in their legs and the extent of their vision.

this sport with a modest investment. After all, the whole point of backpacking is to carry as little as you can safely get away with, not only because every pound in the pack exacts a toll from your enjoyment of the trail, but because the more gadgets you bring into the woods, the harder it is to hear its heartbeat. The analogy of a backpacker as a man with his house on his back may be an apt one, but the Earth provides your living quarters, porch and bathroom, and the rest of the house is best furnished with Shaker austerity.

THE HOUSE

Choosing Your Backpack

Because it serves as the suspension system for your load, the backpack is the most important piece of equipment you'll purchase, as well as the most expensive. There are two basic designs: the **external frame,** which consists of metal bars to which the pack bag attaches, and **internal frame,** which depends on support from metal or composite stays and/or a flexible plastic frame incorporated into the pack.

External Frame: Pros and Cons

External-frame packs are lighter in weight than comparable-sized internal-frame packs. The framework holds the pack bag away from your back, allowing air circulation to cool your skin. External frames have fewer adjustments and the load rides high up, directly over your hips. They also are cheaper; a good-quality one costs about half as much as a top-of-the-line internal-frame model.

On the down side, the top of an external-frame pack rides quite high over your shoulders, and, because the pack frame has no give, it tends to sway back and forth as you walk. The high center of gravity can throw you off-balance, which has obvious dangers in mountainous ter-

Select the Right Size

To carry a week's worth of gear and food, select an internal-frame pack with a capacity of 4,500 to 6,000 cubic inches, or an external frame with 4,000 to 5,000 cubic inches. (External-frame packs can be a bit smaller because they have more room for lashing gear that doesn't fit into the pack bag.) There are some behemoth packs on the market, with up to 7,000 cubic inches carrying capacity, but they are overkill for all but the biggest men. Even Appalachian Trail hikers don't need that much room, for seldom is it necessary to carry more than a week's supply of food before restocking. I often take weekend trips with a 3,600 cubic inch pack bag and my gear doesn't seem cramped for space.

rain, and the pack is prone to catching on rocks and branches when you stray from developed trails.

Internal Frame: Pros and Cons

Internal-frame packs hug the body and provide a lower, more natural center of gravity, which helps stabilize the load during steep climbs. Flexible stays move in synchronization with your body's walking rhythm, adding an extra measure of comfort. On rough ground, or for mountain climbing and cross-country skiing, an internal-frame pack is really the only way to go.

However, the internal frame's sophisticated suspension system comes at both a higher weight and price. Lightweight, inexpensive models are not nearly as good as external-frame packs for supporting heavy loads. Internal-frame packs are also harder to adjust for fit and you must be more careful loading them to maintain the proper weight distribution. They also make your back sweat more, but except for hikes in very hot weather, I've found that a small price to pay for their advantages.

Internal-frame packs hug body contours and provide a lower, more natural center of gravity than external-frame packs. But don't skimp on quality: cheap internal frames won't support heavy loads as well as the external frames on inexpensive packs.

Backpack Buying Tips

The most crucial aspect of pack buying is getting a good fit. Don't walk into an outfitting store with your mind set on a particular brand, because a make that fits one body type exceptionally well may not suit others. Find an experienced salesperson who can help you. If you order

> ### A Woman's Choice
>
> For many years, pack makers never considered altering the dimensions of their product to fit hikers who didn't inherit an XY chromosome. All that has changed, and today women don't have to settle for a man's pack, which is typically too long and has shoulder straps set too far apart. Most manufacturers offer models that are specifically designed for a woman's narrower shoulders, shorter torsos, and smaller waists. One of these models can also be a good choice for a slightly built man or a child.

from the L.L. Bean catalog, pay attention to the torso measurements so you will get the correct size. I once went hiking with an editor from New York who stood five foot nothing in her hiking boots, and who carried a pack that had been engineered for men who stood from 5′ 10″ to 6′ 4″, which was clearly marked on the frame. When she buckled the hip belt, the top of the pack towered over her head by almost two feet! To avoid tipping over, she eventually undid the belt and carried all 50 pounds of equipment on her shoulders. Had she not been one of the toughest people I've known, I doubt she would have made it more than a mile down the trail.

When choosing an external-frame pack, look for a shelf extension at the bottom of the frame, which provides a platform for lashing down gear and helps support heavy loads. An extension at the top of the frame comes in handy for lashing down sleeping pads or other lightweight, bulky gear. It's nice to have a few external pockets and a zippered hood to store maps, trail snacks, water bottles, etc. But many experienced hikers frown on divided compartments inside the pack bag as an unnecessary hindrance to packing.

A couple of final tips: Never buy a pack from the store without trying it on with a full load, and forget about any backpack that doesn't include a fully padded hip belt. Once you do buy your backpack, load it with 40 pounds or so of *clean* gear and walk around with it for several miles. If you can't get the load to ride comfortably, take the pack back and look for another one.

THE BEDROOM: CHOOSING YOUR SHELTER

"Under most conditions," Colin Fletcher wrote in *The Complete Walker,* "the best roof for your bedroom is the sky." This erudite Welshman, whose book remains the "bible" on backpacking more than 30 years after its publication,

The best roof for your bedroom is the sky. On a clear night, the mesh ceiling of this tent lets you count the stars as you fall asleep.

almost never used a tent on his worldwide journeys and was a minimalist in other ways as well: Although he conceded the necessity of boots for rough terrain, above the line of his socks, his concept of the perfect hiking attire was the skin God gave him.

Most of us prefer wearing clothes on the trail and feel more secure having some sort of roof over our heads, but the rule of thumb should be to pack a shelter that is as light and airy as weather conditions—and insects—permit.

The Versatile Tarp

The simplest, lightest, and most versatile shelter is a tarp. The best tarps are made from ripstop, coated nylon, or clear plastic Visqueen (sold in hardware stores). The vinyl tarps sold in discount stores tear at the mere whisper of the word "sharp." But crafting a tarp out of nylon or Visqueen sheeting is very simple. A 6′×6′ square offers minimal coverage for one person; an 8′×8′ square weighs only a few ounces more and can cover two people. For a few dollars you can purchase the materials for the tarp, plus a grommet tool and grommets for making attachments at all four corners and at intervals along each side.

Tarps can be rigged in a number of ways, depending upon the weather conditions and availability of trees (see illustration).

Four ways to rig a tarp. Extend cord between trees for support (A and C), or drape tarp over a log with one end raised (B) for maximum protection against rain or snow. Extend cord from center of tarp to overhanging tree limb (D) for shade in hot weather.

Tarps are all you need for fair-weather backpacking in areas where mosquitoes aren't too troublesome. Transparent Visqueen tarps are a little bulkier than nylon tarps, are less than half the weight of most two-man tents, and give you the advantage of being able to count the stars on your glissade into sleep.

The downside is that tarps do not offer reliable protection in prolonged downpours and must be properly rigged to withstand even moderate rains in windy conditions. You'll need a ground cloth to keep the underside of your sleeping bag clean and dry, which bumps up the weight of the bedroom another few ounces. And tarps aren't as warm as tents.

Bivouac Sacks

A bivouac sack ("bivy," in backpacking parlance) is nothing more than a roomy, weatherproof covering for a sleeping bag. On clear nights, you look up

Bivouac ("bivy") sacks are a lightweight alternative to tents for solo backpackers. Sacks that are supported by a pole are a few ounces heavier, but provide more head room for waiting out a storm.

at the moon; when it rains, you pull the hood of the bivy over your head. Because condensation can be a problem in such confined sleeping quarters, a breathable Gore-Tex shell is more comfortable than coated nylon. A two-layer hood with an interior mosquito netting is a good option during warm, buggy months.

A bivy sack weighs from 1 to 2½ pounds, depending on fabric and structure. Heavier bivys sometimes include a single pole that bends in an arc over the occupant's head, creating a little more room to turn around in.

Bivouac bags are a good way to go on solo trips where every ounce counts, or as a fall-back option during long-distance treks where you plan to spend most nights in hard-sided shelters.

Tents

Most backpacking tents are of a hoop or modified dome design. They use a support system of aluminum, shock-corded poles that attach to clips or thread through sleeves in the outside fabric of the tent. Construction is two layered—the tent itself is breathable nylon with mesh panels for ventilation; the fly is a separate covering layer that has been treated to keep out rain and snow.

Tents rated as one-season offer superior ventilation for summer hiking. Three-season tents strike a balance between adequate ventilation and protection from the elements during spring and fall. Four-season or winter tents are supported by more poles for a given size and are more sturdily constructed, to withstand howling winds and heavy snow. This type of tent is a must for serious mountaineering, but too much of a good thing, and too heavy, for most backpacking.

Summer tents are typically the lightest in weight. I have a one-man Marmot tent that weighs less than two pounds and has kept me bone dry through many high-country storms. But a coffin has more elbow room, and its occupant has no need to roll over in the middle of the night. Most solo tents weigh from 3 to 5 pounds; two-man tents weigh from 4 to 7 pounds. But take those capacity ratings tent manufacturers use with a pinch of salt. Two backpackers will usually be a lot more comfortable in a three-man tent than a two-man tent. You need extra room for your gear, and sometimes your pack as well,

Tents for winter backpacking are more sturdily constructed than three-season tents, with extra poles for support against winds and heavy snow. The fly should be pegged taut for best protection.

The Vestibule: A Mudroom for Your Tent

A vestibule is an extra space at one end of the tent where you can drop your boots, store extra gear, or cook in bad weather. Usually the vestibule is integrated into the fly, so you can lie inside the tent and still have some overhead protection for your stove, which is set outside on the ground. This is a good feature in any tent, but a must in the Pacific Northwest or other areas where you are likely to spend mealtimes under shelter.

during rainy nights. Many tents are dual-rated (as two- to three-man, for example); unless you and your partners are of small stature, use the lower number as your guide. The only certain way of getting the right size tent is to crawl inside it with the number of companions and amount of gear that would accompany you on a trip.

The most important consideration in selecting a tent is weather. Large ventilation panels are crucial for hot-weather camping. A generously cut fly may be the most important component in rainy country; some flies are so skimpy they won't protect the tent from a slanting rain. Generally speaking, the more poles a tent has, the sturdier it will be in a wind. But a ground-hugging, aerodynamic design also helps to stabilize a tent that is subjected to high winds.

Tenting Tips

- Choose a free-standing tent over one that can't be pitched until the corners are staked down. It's easier to erect and can be moved around until you find exactly the right place to set it.

- Many backpacking tents give you the option of pitching the fly and leaving the tent at home. You can save weight on fair-weather trips and use the fly over the pole system as a tarp.

- Best-quality tents have tub-style floors, with the flooring material extending a couple inches onto the sides. But inside seams still need to be sealed to make them fully waterproof. Buy a tube of seam sealer at the outfitters and follow the instructions closely.

- Because it's easy to lose a stake or have it bend out of shape, carry a few extras in your pack. Hard-alloy aluminum stakes with a twisted design hold soft ground best, but it's wise to take along a couple of thin, round stakes, which are easier to work between the stones in rocky soils.

Sleeping Bags

The most practical design of sleeping bag for the backpacker is the mummy bag, which is cut more narrowly at the feet than at the shoulders and incorporates a drawstring hood. Mummy bags hug the body, retaining body heat more efficiently than roomier bags. They also weigh less and take up less space in the pack than rectangular bags. However, mummy bags can feel cramped if you are used to a roomier bag or toss and turn during the night. Some makers offer a compromise—bags that are slightly contoured to body shape but more fully proportioned than conventional mummy design. A few specialty bags open three ways, offering a light inner layer for warm weather with the option of folding over a heavier layer when nights turn crisp.

No matter what style you choose, the major decision you'll have to make is choice of filling material. Both goose down and synthetic offer distinct advantages.

Goose Down: Pros and Cons

Ounce for ounce, down remains the best insulating filler for sleeping bags, despite advances made in synthetic fillers over the past couple decades. Another big advantage is that a down bag stuffs into a smaller stuff sack than a

Rectangular bags (top) are roomier, but most backpackers choose mummy-style bags, which are lighter in weight, retain body heat more efficiently, and take up less room in the pack.

Stuff-Sack Woes

The stuff sacks that come with many (make that most) sleeping bags are too small. Consider purchasing a larger stuff sack—it will make packing your gear a lot easier. If you are worried about space in your backpack, buy a compression sack (sold with some L.L. Bean bags) with side straps that cinch tight to reduce the size of bag.

---

synthetic bag with comparable insulating value. Down also maintains its loft with repeated use and cleaning much longer than synthetic fillers.

The biggest drawback? It's worthless when wet. How important this is depends on where you backpack. On an extended trip in Pacific Northwest, for example, the accumulation of moisture from the atmosphere and your own body can tip the odds in favor of synthetics.

Synthetics: Pros and Cons

The best synthetic bags are about a third less expensive than down bags and maintain their insulative value when wet. In the event of some unforeseen catastrophe, where all your gear becomes soaked and you can't build a fire, a synthetic bag could save your life. Synthetic bags also dry more quickly than down bags and are easier to care for.

Negatives include weight, bulk, and durability. But the gap in performance is steadily narrowing, and today you can order a best-quality synthetic bag from L.L. Bean or other makers that weighs only a half pound or so more than a comparably rated down bag. Synthetics are making converts of serious backpackers every day.

If you're not in bear or mosquito country, who says you have to zip up your tent every night? Sleeping with the door open promotes air circulation, reduces condensation, and helps keep you cool if your sleeping bag has too much insulation.

Temperature Ratings and Weight

Most three-season bags have a temperature rating of about 20° Fahrenheit and weigh between 2½ pounds and 4 pounds for best-quality goose down, or from 3 to 5 pounds for synthetic fillers. That's a good choice for most backpackers in temperate latitudes. Warm-weather bags, rated to 40° F. are little lighter but less versatile. Bags rated at 0° or 20° below may be a better choice for winter backpackers, but they weigh more, take up more pack space, and aren't very comfortable in warm weather.

Second Skins

Breathable fabric liners made of silk, nylon, or polypropylene help keep the inside of a sleeping bag clean and prolong its life. *Fleece liners* extend the comfort range of your bag by 15° or so and can stand alone as a lightweight bag for warm-weather outings. *Vapor-barrier liners* made from coated nylon trap body heat and moisture, which keeps the inside of your bag dry and extends the comfort range without adding more than a few ounces to your pack. Vapor-barrier liners can feel clammy, but are a good idea on addition on winter trips where moisture accumulation can reduce the effectiveness of your sleeping bag.

All these liners fit *inside* the bag. They are sold commercially, but anyone who can work the foot pedal of a sewing machine can easily custom-fit one from material bought at a fabric store.

Temperature ratings can be misleading. There is no industry standard, so one maker's bag that's rated to 20°F. may sleep much warmer than another's. People are not created equal, either. Put two hikers into identical bags and one will be cold, the other one hot. This makes it hard to choose when you don't have the opportunity of trying out a sleeping bag before buying. I suspect that many neophytes are seduced by a low temperature rating and buy a bag that's warmer than what they need. You can wear extra clothing or add a liner to extend the comfort range of the bag, but you can't very well take out some of the stuffing to make your bag sleep cooler.

Sleeping Bag Buying Tips

All fillers are not created equal. If you choose down, insist on goose down (as opposed to duck down, or a combination of down and feathers). If you go with a synthetic bag, be wary of a cheap price tag. Synthetic filler materials vary greatly in quality; the poorer ones will lose their loft and insulative value more rapidly than the fillers in a more expensive bag. Most quality bags incorporate a hood and an interior zipper lining, called a draft tube, to keep heat from escaping at the side. Winter bags, as well as some three-season models, have a draft collar and a system of drawstrings at the neck and the edges of the hood for maximum insulation.

Most makers, including L.L. Bean, offer bags cut for a woman's body proportions, which also can be good choices for children and smaller men. Some models can be zipped together to create a double bag.

Always err on the side of buying a bag that's cut a little generously. Remember that on cold nights you might want to add an inside liner or bring some of your gear inside the bag, which will take up additional space.

Care for Sleeping Bags

Each time you wash your sleeping bag, you reduce its loft and longevity, so wait until your bag is as filthy as you can stand before cleaning it. Next to handing your bag over to an backpacking outfitter for professional cleaning, the best method is simply to hand wash the bag with gentle detergent in a bathtub of warm water. Appropriate cleansers are sold in sporting goods stores. A simpler alternative, though slightly more damaging to the bag, is to use a large, front-loading washing machine at a laundromat. After washing, dry the bag on the cool setting for a couple hours. You also can air dry the bag outside by draping it across several boards or clotheslines stretched parallel to each other.

Never store a sleeping bag in a stuff sack at home. Use a large pillowcase (some L.L. Bean bags come with over-sized storage bags) or loosely fold the sleeping bag in a dry room of your house.

Sleeping Pads

Sleeping pads have two purposes: to insulate your body from the cold and to provide cushioning between your sleeping bag and the ground. Backpackers have the choice of two basic designs: closed-cell pads and self-inflating foam mattresses.

Closed-cell Pads: Pros and Cons

Thin, *closed-cell pads* come in a variety of styles—single layer, ridged, air-bob, even accordion-style for easy folding. For a few dollars they perform the function of insulation admirably, but most are not much more forgiving than the ground underneath them. They weigh next to nothing, but they don't roll up compactly and often wind up being lashed to the outside of the pack, where they are exposed to rain and sharp branches, unless you cover them with a stuff sack.

Self-inflating foam mattresses come in various lengths and lofts and offer the most comfortable foundation for a good night's sleep.

Self-inflating Foam Mattresses: Pros and Cons

Don't confuse self-inflating foam mattresses with the air mattresses familiar to car campers. The latter are far too heavy for backpacking, are prone to puncture, and have no insulating value. Self-inflating foam mattresses inflate with a twist of an air valve to a thickness of from ¾ inch to 2 inches. Therm-A-Rest invented this design and their mattresses remain the most popular. The ¾ length is the most popular backpacking size (except in winter, when a full-length mattress is preferable). Self-inflating foam mattresses roll up compactly and are extremely comfortable. Their Achilles heel is weight (from 1 to 3 pounds), which most veteran backpackers will gladly suffer for the restorative value of a good night's sleep. The other disadvantage is cost—about three times as much as a closed-cell pad. Take the hit on your checkbook. You won't be sorry.

A Place to Lay Your Head

Blow-up and self-inflating pillows are widely available through outfitters. But most pillows you'll see in the backcountry are makeshift affairs—typically, a stuff sack filled with the clothes the backpacker isn't wearing to bed. The colder the night, the thinner the pillow. To add comfort without packing additional weight, slip a cotton T-shirt over the stuff sack or pack extra clothes in a flannel pillowcase. An empty water bag, partially inflated, makes an excellent pillow.

THE KITCHEN

Backpacking Stoves

There are still places where backpackers can build small cooking fires, discreetly disperse the coals, and do no harm to the forest floor. However, along many trails building fires is either prohibited or environmentally damaging. In any case, cooking on a stove is cleaner and more efficient. Backpacking stoves can be broadly categorized by the types of fuel they burn.

Refillable, Liquid Fuel Stoves: Pros and Cons

These are the work horses for most backpackers, especially in cold weather, where canister stoves that burn propane or butane lose efficiency. Not very long ago, most liquid fuel stoves ran on one type of fuel only, so you had to chose among white gasoline, kerosene, and alcohol. White gasoline (most commonly sold as Coleman fuel) is the most efficient fuel, burning with a very hot flame, even in cold weather. Kerosene was the choice for intrepid backpackers, since it was available throughout the world. However, kerosene stoves are more difficult to prime and ignite than white gas stoves. Alcohol is the only liquid fuel that burns unpressurized, making it safer to use in tent vestibules during winter trips or on rainy days. But it only produces about half the heat of white gas and you need more of it, which adds weight to your pack.

Today, the best backpacking stoves are labeled "multifuel" and will burn white gas, unleaded gasoline, kerosene, or, in emergencies, diesel fuel or dry cleaning fluid.

Many liquid fuel stoves, like the popular MSR series, operate with a detachable fuel tank. Other stoves have an integral fuel tank underneath the burner. The latter can be more dangerous if used in confined spaces, where heat buildup can "blow" the pressure valve, releasing a streak of flame. Don't surround them with rocks or operate them in a hole and you won't have a problem.

Most liquid-fuel stoves need to be primed, a feature that may scare some novice backpackers into making other choices. It shouldn't. The operation consists of three simple steps: 1) Pump the stove to pressurize the fuel; 2) preheat the fuel cup with a dribble of gas or a strip of priming paste and light with a match; 3) after the fuel cup is hot, open the valve and you have lift-off. In fact, lift-off isn't a bad choice of words to describe the heat output of a dual-fuel stove. These stoves make boiling water for coffee or freeze-dried

Most serious backpackers depend upon a liquid fuel stove with a detachable fuel bottle for camp cooking.

dinners a cinch. However, many stoves have only two flame adjustments: dead out and blast furnace. You can't turn the flame down for simmering. If you need this feature, look for a stove such as the Peak 1 Apex 11, which weighs more than some other popular models but does permit adjustment of the flame.

Canister Stoves: Pros and Cons

Canister stoves burn pressurized gas, usually butane or butane/propane mixture. Many novices are seduced by the ease of operation—light a match, slightly open the valve until the flame catches, and you're off and cooking. Simmering is no problem. The stoves are extremely lightweight and come in two designs: those that have a separate fuel canister that reattaches via a nozzle for each use, and those that you attach once and then leave in place until the canister is empty. The former are less bulky to pack and give you the option of changing canisters when the fuel pressure begins to drop and heat output fades.

Another advantage of canister stoves is price. They typically cost from a third to half as much as liquid-fuel stoves.

On the down side, canister stoves work poorly in temperatures below 40° Fahrenheit, the flame isn't as hot as white gas, and as the pressure in the canister drops, the heat output may fall below that needed to boil water. But for warm-weather backpacking, canister stoves are an attractive alternative.

Solid-Fuel Stoves

Stoves that operate on fuel pellets or the *Zzip* stove, which uses a battery-operated fan to circulate air as it burns twigs and pine cones, have the twin benefits of light weight and little bulk. I carry a tiny, fold-up aluminum stove that will boil a cup of water with a single fuel pellet. This stove is ideal on long day-hikes for making a cup of afternoon tea or instant soup, but for day-in, day-out backpack cooking, solid-fuel stoves are a poor choice. They also may be technically illegal where making fires is prohibited.

Cookware

Unless you are planning elaborate meals, all your culinary needs in the backcountry can be covered with a spoon, a cup, a pocket knife, and a 1-quart pot with a lid. (A 2-quart pot is best for parties of two or three hikers). The best pots are made of titanium or aluminum/steel al-

---

Tips on Stove Use

- Check all stove attachments (fuel tanks, canisters, caps, control knobs) before lighting.
- Use an eyedropper to transfer gas from your fuel tank to the fuel cup for priming.
- Liquid-fuel tanks operate best when more than half full, but don't fill them to the brim. The fuel needs room to expand under pressure for the stove to operate properly.
- Never remove a nondetachable butane/propane canister until it's completely empty.
- In breezy weather, protect the flame of your stove with a windbreak such as a circle of tall rocks. Shiny heat reflectors (if your stove doesn't come with one, make one out of heavy aluminum foil) also improve performance.
- Keep liquid-fuel bottles and propane/butane canisters warm by placing them in the foot of your sleeping bag on cold nights.
- Stoves run best on clean, pure fuel. You can filter out some impurities with a fine wire mesh, sold in backpacking outfitters.
- Transporting fuel is prohibited on airlines, so make sure you know where to purchase some before hitting the trail.

loy, but aluminum pots are lightweight and serviceable, if you don't mind the slight metallic flavor they impart to food or the possible health risks reported with aluminum. Many pots have lids that double as frying pans or plates, but a tin pie plate serves the purpose just as well. A few 18-inch squares of heavy-duty aluminum foil will cook any windfalls of nature that come your way, such as fresh-caught trout from an alpine lake. A featherweight plastic bowl that nestles inside the pot does double duty as a plate or a bowl for soup and cereal.

Two words of warning: Beware of thin metal cups. They conduct heat and can scald the skin off your lips. And buy one of those little pot grabbers that look like pliers to move your pot on and off the burner.

BUYING SECONDHAND

Backpacking is a way of life that separates the chaff from the wheat. As hikers upgrade their gear or drop off the trail, their equipment winds up in garage sales and secondhand, outdoor specialty stores. One chain of stores that specializes in this market is Play It Again Sports (call 1–800–433–2540 to locate a store in your area), which has franchises throughout the United States and Canada. These are great places to shop for bargains, but you have to be careful. Outdated gear is often heavier than newer equipment. Never buy a tent without erecting it first to be sure everything's there and everything works.

The synthetic fill in sleeping bags breaks down and loses much of its efficiency with wear. Only consider bags that retain their loft and have silky smooth, two-way zippers.

Many older backpacks have skimpy belt systems. Load a prospective pack with gear, check all the adjusting straps, and walk around the store or yard with it for 20 minutes or more before reaching for the green.

Closed-cell pads can be picked up for pennies in yard sales. Buy one even if you use a different pad to sleep on. Cut out an 18-inch square, strap it onto the outside of your pack, and use it as a seat during rest stops. Buying a self-inflating foam mattress entails more risk. It may have a slow valve leak that is difficult to diagnose in a secondhand store or yard sale.

Unless you know liquid-fuel backpacking stoves inside and out, save your money for a new model that uses dual fuel. Canister stoves have fewer working parts to break and are usually sold for low prices, anyway. But don't buy the stove unless you know the right canisters are still available.

On rocky trails like this one it's important to watch your step, especially with the weight of a heavy pack on your back.

New backpacking gear is moderately expensive, but a complete outfit can still be bought for the cost of a few nights in a seaside motel, and good gear will last just about as long as your bones can get you into the hills. The virtues of bargain equipment can be overrated. Choose the lightest, most up-to-date gear you can afford.

CHAPTER 7

Shouldering the Load

"What does he care if he hasn't any money, he doesn't need any money, all he needs is his rucksack with those little plastic bags of dried food and a good pair of shoes and off he goes and enjoys the privileges of a millionaire . . ."

JACK KEROUAC

After a couple days on the trail, loading up a pack in the morning takes little forethought. Everything has its place and a few minutes after striking the tent, you're ready to go. The same procedure, undertaken at the trailhead before you start to hike, can entail a half-hour struggle and exhaust a hailstorm of four-letter words. Save yourself the frustration by setting aside a block of time at home to practice and become familiar with your gear.

Is the vista worth the climb? The answer may depend upon how efficient you are at weeding out unnecessary gear and distributing the load in your pack.

PRE-PACKING

One of the keys to efficient packing is to make every item pack-ready before-hand. Many veterans use a system of color-coded stuff sacks to separate equipment into groups: clothing, emergency gear, food, and so on. It's important to use a coated nylon stuff sack to add a measure of water-repellency for your sleeping bag, or else line the inside of the stuff sack with a plastic trash bag. You also can use plastic trash bags to store extra clothes (tall kitchen bags are a good size for this purpose). In rainy climates, some backpackers line the inside of the pack bag with a large plastic sack.

Keep an eye out for ways to reduce bulk and protect fragile gear. You can accomplish both goals, for example, by slipping your camera into a fleece cap and cradling it inside the cookpot.

Repackage food such as dry cereal, box soup mixes, jerky, and dried fruit into reclosable plastic bags. Store peanut butter, honey, cooking oil, and margarine in refillable, plastic squeeze tubes, available at the local outfitters. Clear plastic 35mm film canisters are excellent for storing small items such as instant coffee or salt and pepper mix, but either wash them thoroughly first to remove the chemical residue or line the inside with a small plastic bag. Never carry glass into the backcountry and be certain to double-bag any items that might leak.

PACKING AN EXTERNAL-FRAME PACK

In backpacking, you want the load to center over your hips and feet. External-frame packs ride higher than internal-frame packs and tilt forward over your head at the upper end; for this reason, the heaviest gear should be placed high in the pack bag and as close to the frame as possible.

Because of its bulk and light weight, the sleeping bag is secured to the bottom of the frame with the straps located directly under the pack bag. Many backpackers tuck their rolled-up sleeping pad between the sleeping bag and the pack bag, although some prefer to lash it to the back or on top of the pack. Place clothing, poncho, or rain gear on top of the sleeping bag and top off with the heavier items, including cooking gear and food bag. Load the side pockets evenly to avoid listing to port or starboard as you hike. The tent is usually the heaviest piece of gear and is customarily lashed to the top of the frame at the back of your head.

An external-frame pack loaded in this fashion is top-heavy, but it will ride more comfortably than one with the heavy items placed on the bottom. How-

ever, when you are negotiating steep terrain, it's a good
idea to redistribute the load
to bring the center of gravity
closer to your back and hips.
It will pull at your shoulders
more, but you will be less
likely to lose your balance
and fall.

> ### Gender Bending: Tips for Balancing a Woman's Pack
>
> The center of gravity for most men is near the dia-phragm. A woman's relatively shorter torso and longer legs places her center of gravity lower, down around the hips. For this reason, top-heavy packs feel unstable to some women. Many female back-packers report that they achieve a better sense of equilibrium by placing heavy gear near the bottom of the pack.

PACKING AN INTERNAL-FRAME PACK

With an internal-frame pack, the sleeping bag is wedged into the bottom of
the pack sack to hold it open, giving the pack definition. I like to fold my
sleeping pad and stuff it down inside the pack sack against the flexible panel
of the internal frame. This puts a soft cushion next to my back and insulates
the gear and food bag from body heat.

Because an internal-frame pack hugs the body and rides lower than an external-frame pack, many backpackers feel it balances better with a lower center of gravity. When climbing, place the heaviest gear down low and as close
to the small of your back as possible, in order to distribute the weight over
your hips. On easy trails, you
may feel more comfortable
with the weight up high.

Tightening the compres-
sion straps along the sides
will draw the load closer to
your body.

ADJUSTING YOUR PACK FOR FIT

Fitting an external-frame pack
is relatively simple. Lift both
shoulders to pull the pack
high, then cinch the waist
belt. The waist belt should

> ### Packing Tips
>
> - Gear that you need along the trail should be readily accessible. Lunch foods, water bottle, a warm jacket and rain gear should either be lashed to out-side tabs, placed in the top of the pack bag, or stuffed into external pockets.
>
> - Maps, sunscreen, insect repellent, journal and pen-cil, toilet paper, and foot-care items can be zipped into the flap compartment of an internal-frame pack for easy access.
>
> - Cushion sharp items with clothing to keep them from puncturing other gear or pack fabric.
>
> - Separate cookstove and fuel bottle from gear or food that could take on its odors. Pack fuel bottle right side up, preferably in a side pocket.

To heft a pack, grasp the tops of the loosened shoulder straps with both hands.

Swing the pack onto your thigh or hip. Set heavy packs on a rock or log before lifting.

ride over and just above the iliac crest, which is the bony part of the hip you feel at your sides. Tighten the shoulder straps to transfer some of the weight off your hips. You want them snug, but not so tight that they will cut into you. Cinch the sternum strap and you're ready to hike.

Because the adjusting harness of an internal-frame pack is built into the suspension system, adjusting for proper fit is a little more complex. Cinch the hip-belt, then the hip belt stabilizer straps. You should be able to slip a finger underneath the straps; if you can't, they're too tight. Cinch the shoulder straps so that they are snug. Tighten the load-adjuster straps, which are located near the tops of the shoulder straps. This pulls the top of the pack against your body, transferring the weight from your shoulders to your hips. Cinch the sternum strap.

The harness on some internal-frame packs adjusts for torso length. The shoulder straps should be attached to the packbag a couple of inches lower than the tops of the shoulders. The load-adjuster straps should be positioned at an angle of 10 to 45 degrees above the horizontal, attaching to the pack several inches above the tops of the shoulders (see illustration on page 106).

Slip an arm into shoulder strap. Using the pack's momentum, shift weight onto your back.

Slip the other arm into the opposite shoulder strap.

Cinch belt and adjust straps so that they rest comfortably on your shoulders.

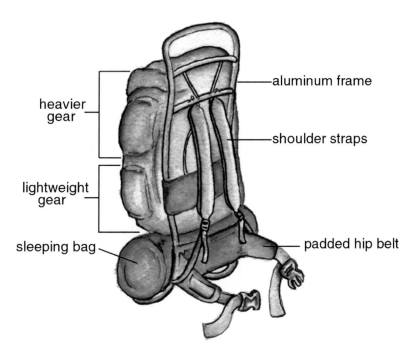

External frame pack

top pocket

load adjuster straps
(see illustration below)

lightweight
gear

side compression
straps

heavier
gear

sleeping
bag

shoulder
straps

sternum
strap

padded
hip belt

hip-belt
stabilizer strap

Internal frame pack

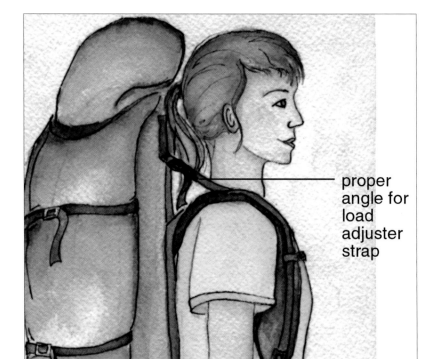

proper
angle for
load
adjuster
strap

To adjust pack harness for fit, position shoulder straps so that they lightly cup your shoulders. Load adjuster straps should be positioned at an angle of 10 to 45 degrees above the horizontal.

A MATTER OF WEIGHT: THE 25-PERCENT SOLUTION

Now that you have your fully loaded pack properly adjusted, with about 90 percent of the weight on your hips, walk around for a few minutes. You should be in your living room or backyard at this point, *not at the trailhead!* Be honest with yourself. Can you carry this much weight comfortably for five or six hours every day?

If you harbor any doubts, step up onto the bathroom scales. Then take the pack off and weigh yourself again. Do the math. Most backpacking authorities recommend that a man carry no more than one-third of his body weight, a woman, who typically has an edge in endurance but less bone and muscle mass, no more than one quarter of her weight. In fact, most of us won't enjoy a backpacking trip if we burden ourselves with this heavy a load.

A pack that weighs from one fifth to one quarter of your body weight is much more reasonable to carry. That means that a 165-pound man should pare away at his load until it weighs no more than 40 pounds; a 120-pound woman should try carry no more than 30 pounds.

If your load is too heavy, start the process of elimination with clothing. Remember this rule of thumb: you need enough insulating layers to keep you reasonably warm while being reasonably active during the coldest weather you can expect. In camp, or while resting, you can always use a sleeping bag, rain gear, or space blankets to cut the chill. So get rid of the extra sweater, the third pair of socks, and the second pair of underwear, and substitute light-weight sandals for heavy camp shoes.

Empty the food bag and separate packages into days on the trail. Eliminate anything that's left over, or anything that provides marginal nutrition in relation to its extra weight, such as an apple. Put the metal utensils back in the kitchen drawer and substitute plastic. Set aside the backup flashlight; if the main one should fail, the worst that can happen is you'll have to spend a night in the dark, just as your ancestors did for the last four million years. Ditto for the second pair of sunglasses. Consider exchanging the water filter pump for a small vial of iodine tablets. Do you really need a squeeze tube of biodegradable soap? A GPS unit? The fleece liner for the sleeping bag? The pack cover? Nah.

I once went backpacking into Montana's Pintlar Wilderness with a woman who carried a cell phone and four liters of Diet Coke among about 30 pounds of excess clothing and gear. Every morning, we climbed to the top of a ridge so she could try to call her husband, who was a Wall Street broker. She never got through, but she did consume the diet Coke. That brought the excess baggage down to about 26 pounds. She describes the trip as "memorable." Enjoyable it was not.

Trimming pack contents is a ruthless process and you're going to have to sacrifice some creature comforts. But carrying a light load is probably the most important thing you can do to increase your enjoyment of the outing.

HEADING OUT

The best way to prepare for the trail is to carry your backpack around town an hour or so every other day for a month or so before your trip. No backpacker I know has ever done this. Life is too complicated and the first mile of the trail for most of us will be the first time we've carried a heavy load since the last backpacking trip.

Try to get as early a start as possible so you don't have to rush. Select a trail that offers good camping sites within four to six miles of the trailhead and keep elevation gain to a minimum. That allows you plenty of time for pitching camp, cooking supper, and relaxing before bedtime, and gives you an adequate period for recovery before the next leg of the trip.

Go at your own pace. There's an old saying among backpackers: "Hike your own hike." If your companions want to go faster, make a plan to meet at a specified spot down the trail.

In one crucial way, the first few miles are the most dangerous of the trip: This is when your feet are most susceptible to blistering. It doesn't matter how many hours you have put on your boots in previous seasons. Boots change in size and stiffness according to weather conditions and even your feet change, not just from one year to the next, but with changes in temperature and the weight you are packing.

Stop at the first hint of irritation, take off your boots and socks, and examine your skin for hot spots. A hot spot will appear slightly red (like a mild burn) when rubbed. Bring out your blister kit (it should always be packed where it's easy to get to) and cover the hot spot and surrounding skin with a strip of athletic tape,

Covering a "hot spot" with moleskin and/or athletic tape will help prevent blistering farther down the trail.

moleskin, or even duct tape. Some hikers cut out a hole in the moleskin and place it directly over the hot spot. If you catch the hot spot early enough, these initial measures may be enough to stave off a blister.

If you do develop a full-fledged blister, don't despair. With proper treatment, you'll still be able to walk on it, though the shorter the distance is to your first camp,

> **Tips for Blister Prevention**
>
> - Keep toenails trimmed short.
> - Check socks for creases.
> - Wear synthetic sock liners to trap friction between fabric layers.
> - Keep your feet dry by changing socks every couple of hours. Drape the worn pair over your backpack to air dry along the trail.
> - Place moleskin or strips of tape on the backs of your heels before starting the hike, especially in rainy weather. Wet skin is most prone to blistering.

the better. First, lance the blister with a sterilized needle (to sterilize, heat the needle with the flame of a butane lighter). Then coat the blister with Spenco 2nd Skin, a slippery, gel-like substance that acts as a moisture barrier, and cover the 2nd Skin with a wide strip of tape or moleskin to keep it in place. Adhesive tape will stick much better if you paint your skin first with tincture of benzoin compound. Spenco also offers a complete blister kit that contains the dressing, foam pads, and adhesive sheets.

Backpacking in the Rain

Most breathable raingear made today incorporates a system of zippered vents that help let off steam. They work to a degree, especially in cool weather. But don't let any advertisement convince you that breathable, waterproof fabrics will keep you dry in heavy rain. Even the best fabrics don't pass water vapor at the same rate you generate perspiration, at least while you are exerting under the weight of a pack.

In warm weather, you do have the option of hiking wet. In my experience that is the most comfortable way to travel, although you need to pack dry clothes to change into in camp.

I have never seen a backpacking guide recommend umbrellas, but for steady, windless rain—in other words, standard Pacific Coast weather—an umbrella will keep you drier than the most expensive rain gear. It weighs less than a pound, and if it breaks, you're only out a few bucks.

Remember that chills set in fast when you're wet. Keep a fleece jacket handy for rest stops. If your hands get cold, cover them with plastic bags,

Hiking along the coast, where salt spray on your face can be washed off by rainwater from the sky. Be prepared for inclement weather by wearing Gore-Tex raingear and keep a fleece jacket in your pack to stave off chills.

secured at the wrist by rubber bands. The bags work as well or better than fleece gloves, which would soon be soaked, anyway.

Rest Stops

Resting gives you time to rehydrate with a few swallows of water and stoke your furnace with a handful of trail mix or a strip of jerky. Just as important, it allows the cells

Hints for a Rainy Day

- Wear a wide-brimmed hat. It keeps your face drier than the hood of a parka or rain jacket.
- Lightweight gaiters will help keep your socks and boots dry.
- Consider buying Gore-Tex socks if you will be hiking through a rain forest. Vapor-barrier liners improvised from plastic produce bags will also keep your feet warm if your boots become wet.
- Use a rain cover on your backpack. The ones that attach with stretchy cords fit best.

in your body to flush out the lactic acid that has built up in your thigh and calf muscles while hiking. The re-oxygenated muscles will give you a boost of energy when you resume hiking.

Many backpacking authorities recommend resting for 10 minutes after each 50 minutes of hiking. Shorter stops don't flush out enough lactic acid; longer rests foster day dreaming, conversation, and other forms of procrastination that make for long days. Also, muscles stiffen as they cool down, and the longer you sit, the harder it is to get going and relax back into a comfortable hiking rhythm.

Sometimes, the prospect of lifting and shouldering a heavy pack after a rest stop can be so daunting that it's better just to leave it on. Look for a place where you can rest the bottom of the pack on a log or rock. Take the weight off while you sit by leaving the belt unbuckled and the shoulder straps and chest strap relaxed.

TRAIL ETIQUETTE

As a rule of thumb, yield the trail to faster hikers, bicyclists, and all-terrain vehicles (ATVs). You may disapprove of ATVs in the backcountry, but the place to fight that battle is not on a forest trail where their use is legal. Usually, stepping to the side of the trail and politely nodding or saying hello suffices for proper etiquette.

Horses are another matter. Avoid startling them—they can and will spook for no apparent reason. Get a few yards off the low side of the trail, stand still, and don't talk until they are well past.

Boisterous hikers shatter the serenity and drive away wildlife for others who share the trail. Talk softly and if you are part of a large party, consider breaking into two or three groups to dilute the impact of your presence.

THE REST STEP

The rest step is a method to fall back on when the combination of exhaustion, a heavy pack, and a steep trail slows your progress to a crawl. Hiking until your thighs burn and your heart thumps your sternum strap is neither healthy nor productive, even if you stop every 100 feet or so to bring your pulse rate down. By using the rest step, your body takes a breather with each step and allows you to keep moving forward without gasping like a fish.

The method taught by most mountaineering schools is to keep the weight on your back leg after moving the other uphill. Rest a moment with the weight on your straight rear leg. Then transfer the weight to your uphill leg and take a step with your rear leg. Your legs have now switched position. Pause with your weight on the downhill leg. Repeat.

I find that my companions and I use the rest step most often during that last steep ascent, before the trail levels out near the outlet of the alpine lake where we intend to camp. In a few more minutes, the water will reflect the spreading of weary smiles. And the miles will be forgotten as we struggle out of heavy boots and slip into camp shoes. But that is in a few more minutes. For the time being we labor to put one foot in front of the other, taking our comfort in the thought that the greater our effort now, the greater our reward at the end of the trail.

CHAPTER
8

Minimum-Impact Camping

"All other things being equal,
choose a john with a view."

COLIN FLETCHER

Pitching camp doesn't begin at the end of a long day on the trail. It begins at home, in black and white, with reading backcountry regulations. And it begins with a conscious commitment to respect the land you will live on by learning principles of minimum-impact camping.

Stipulations about where you can erect a tent in the backcountry vary widely. On many public lands, camping within 200 feet of a lake, stream, or trail is prohibited (and should be discouraged everywhere). In some national parks, you must reserve specific backcountry campsites in advance of your trip. Further restrictions may apply. For example, in Yellowstone National Park, you can reserve a backcountry campsite for cooking, but are instructed to walk several hundred feet away from it into the forest to sleep, in order to prevent confrontations with grizzly bears.

If you don't have a copy of backpacking regulations, order one by calling the district office of the land agency.

THE WILDERNESS CAMPSITE

An ideal campsite is easier to describe than it is to find. First, it should be flat, with no rock stubble or roots to trip over or put a crick in your spine while

The rewards of backpacking: a campsite in pristine wilderness miles from the closest road.

you try to sleep. The campsite should have trees or large rocks to shield it from the prevailing wind, yet remain open enough to permit a breeze to keep mosquitoes at bay. A source of clear water is a plus. It's nice to have a log to sit on, and perhaps a flat stone for the stove. A forest floor composed of loose duff, such as the layer of needles found under a pine canopy, is ideal for pitching the tent. It has a soft top layer to ease aching bones, but the earth underneath is firm enough to hold tent stakes. Duff also absorbs water and is less likely to turn into a quagmire of mud should it rain.

What else? An alpine tarn holding the reflection of mountain peaks, trout rising within casting distance of the shore, the lullaby of an inlet stream to sing you to sleep, an eagle's cry upon waking—I have camped in such heavens before.

I have also, through mistakes, learned what to avoid when choosing a wilderness campsite. Ridge tops and open basins, besides being exposed to winds, are more likely to be struck by lightning than sheltered forest. Game trails are tempting, because the hooves of the herds have worn them flat. But I have had the guy ropes to my tent tripped on by elk, and why force a bear to walk around you when you could have camped a few hundred feet downwind, allowing him to pass without even knowing you were near?

Nearly every year, desert flash floods claim the lives of hikers or backpackers. So don't pitch a tent in arroyos or gullies that show indication of previous flooding, even if the sand is dry. Don't camp at the edge of a cliff or the base of a talus slope, where loose rocks could flatten your tent during the night. And in the winter, don't camp below an avalanche chute.

Most of these tips are simple common sense. A little less obvious to novice backpackers is the danger of falling branches or trees. Like forest animals, human beings seldom look up for danger. But the dead or dying trees in an eastern climax forest are called "widow makers" for good reason. In the Rocky Mountains where I live, forest fire and devastation by bark beetles have rusted the needles of large stands of pine trees, many of which still appear strong but will fall over with the push of a hand or a hefty gust of wind. Wherever there is nearly as much wood on the ground as remains standing, choose your campsite carefully.

Second-hand Campsites

Along popular trail systems, always try to camp in a site that shows signs of use by others. An existing site may have drawbacks—uneven ground or mar-

Before pitching camp, make certain that any trees nearby are sturdy enough to withstand strong winds. There's little danger of these vigorous firs falling on the tent.

ring by fire rings, for example—but camping there is preferable to pitching camp on top of untrammeled vegetation. Once destroyed, ground cover can take decades to recover. Established campsites have already been denuded, and as long as you restrict foot traffic to paths leading from the site, further damage to the environment is minimal.

Communal Camping

No one enjoys the prospect of uninvited company after expending a great deal of effort to be alone. In most places, this isn't too much of a problem. You can usually find a site that offers some privacy, whether it entails hiking to the far side of the lake or another mile up the trail. But in some national parks and especially along heavily used eastern trail systems, such as the Appalachian Trail, backpackers are expected to share sites or communal shelters.

If you've done your homework first, this shouldn't come as a surprise. And it shouldn't be the cause of too much concern. Those who camp in communal sites often find stimulating companionship, for fellow hikers are typically people who share your values and love of wild country.

However, backcountry shelters can be crowded during the summer. If a shelter is full when you arrive, or if you pull in long after dark, it's a common courtesy to set up your tent outside. This is a good practice if you plan to get up before dawn, as well, so as not to wake other backpackers. If your party is on the receiving end of company, make hikers welcome by offering to share the shelter, no matter how full it may be already. Most will decline and pitch a tent nearby, but unless you offer, someone who is unprepared to spend a rainy night outside might hike on in the dark rather than impose upon your privacy.

Avoiding the Crowd

For many of us, a backpack is a ticket to solitude. Our idea of a perfect campsite does not include a lakeshore studded with primary colors where others have pitched their tents. One suggestion for getting away from it is to backpack during the off-season, particularly in the autumn, when shorter days, cooler nights (read "fewer bugs") and cloudless skies combine for perfect hiking conditions throughout much of our nation. No matter when you hike, the farther you travel from cities, paved roads, and trailheads, the fewer people you are likely to meet along the trail. And the easiest and quickest way of all to close the curtain of humanity behind you is to leave established trails and strike off cross-country.

Backpacking in winter is rigorous, but there is no better way to beat the summer crowds.

PITCHING CAMP

It's tempting to rest after dropping your pack in a campsite, but after heavy exertion, chills can set in quickly. It's best to get your work out of the way while the sky is blue and your muscles are still warm from hiking.

The first order of business is to divide the site into sections where your pack, kitchen area, and tent will be situated. The kitchen gets the heaviest use and should be located on a surface that can withstand the impact of your boots. A broad, flat stone is best. Mineral soil is the next choice. Composed of sand and studded with small stones or rock chips, it is much more durable than rich, dark organic soil.

For easy access, lean your pack against a rock or tree next to the kitchen. Don't put it where you have to trample vegetation each time you need to dig into the pack sack.

Because the area around your tent suffers comparatively little foot traffic, it can pitched on top of organic soil if no more durable surface is available. If you must set up on vegetation, sedges and grass can withstand much more impact than woody plants with broad leaves. On sloped ground, pitch your tent so that your head will rest slightly uphill.

Stake the tent down over top of the ground cloth, then roll or crumple up the edges of the cloth where they protrude, so that rain water won't

---

Blueprint for Pitching Camp in the Rain

1. After removing the tent bag, drape a poncho or rain cover over your pack top keep the contents dry.
2. Spread out ground cloth and pitch tent with the back toward the wind. Use all the stakes, even if the tent is freestanding.
3. Secure the rain fly, stretching it taut. A sagging rain fly is very inefficient in a storm.
4. Bring your pack inside the tent vestibule, out of the rain. If your tent doesn't have a vestibule, you can jury-rig a tarp or poncho over the tent entrance by tying it off to handy trees.
5. Sit down just inside the mouth of the tent with your boots outside the entrance. Take off your wet boots and set them in the vestibule. Put on camp shoes and don a fleece jacket to stave off chills. Roll out your sleeping pad, but leave the sleeping bag inside its waterproof stuff sack until bedtime.
6. Check to make sure you've battened down all the hatches, then fire up your backpack stove in the vestibule and make a cup of cocoa.
7. Rig a clothesline inside the tent to drape wet socks and shirts. Your body heat will help dry them.
8. If the storm doesn't let up, you can be in for a long evening in close quarters. This is where a good book comes in handy. Though some may think it sacrilege, I once packed a shortwave radio into the mountains and listened to the fifth game of the 1997 World Series while it snowed on the tent. It made for a memorable, and endurable, evening.

run down between the cloth and the tent bottom. Pull the rain fly over the top, using all the guy ropes or elastic cords to stretch the fabric until it is taut.

Roll out and inflate your air mattress, remove your sleeping bag from its stuff bag, fluff it up, and put it inside the tent.

Many backpackers brew a cup of tea or hot cocoa after pitching camp to help stave off the inevitable chill that sets in once you've stopped exercising. While waiting for the water to boil, shrug on a fleece jacket, untie the heavy hiking boots, peel off your damp socks, drape them over a bush to air dry, and change into camp shoes or sandals. More chores will beckon—fetching water, roping a tree limb to hang food from bears, cooking dinner—but try to keep thoughts of work at bay for a while. Relish the tired ache in your body and drink in the beauty of your surroundings.

Filter pumps, though bulky, are the most effective way of removing the **Giardia** *cyst from water gathered from backcountry lakes and steams.*

PURIFYING WATER

The crystal threads of water that race through Montana's Bob Marshall Wilderness look to be among the nation's purest sources of water. Can you drink from them? Sure. Will you get sick? Possibly. If you do, the likely culprit will be *Giardia lamblia,* a water-borne protozoal cyst (spread by animal droppings) that causes severe intestinal cramping and worse—much, much worse.

To avoid contracting giardiasis, you must purify *all* water that does not issue directly from the earth. Boiling is the time-tested method. Simply bringing water to a boil is sufficient to kill the cyst, although at higher altitudes, where water boils at a lower temperature, err on the safe side by boiling the water for several minutes. Some hikers don't care for the taste of boiled water, but it can be improved by *decanting*, a fancy word for pouring the water back and forth between two bottles.

Water can be purified by chemical warfare, too, specifically by adding halogens such as iodine. The tablets must dissolve completely in the water and take some time to act—the colder the water, the longer the purification time, up to half an hour or so. Water treated with iodine tastes like it, but some manufacturers (Potable Aqua, for example) package iodine with a com-

Making a Water Bag

For transporting water to a campsite, the best container by far is a collapsible water bag. You can buy one from a catalog or outfitter, but it's easy to make your own water bag from the silver bag that holds the wine in a 3- or 5-liter wine box. After drinking the wine, remove the bag from the box and pry off the spigot. Rinse the bag thoroughly, then fill it with a solution of water and baking soda and let it sit overnight to remove the wine taste. Sew a tote bag from ripstop nylon, cutting out a hole for the spigot and adding a strap to the top so you can hang the bag from a tree stub. Such a water bag weighs but a couple of ounces, compacts into nothing, and is surprisingly durable.

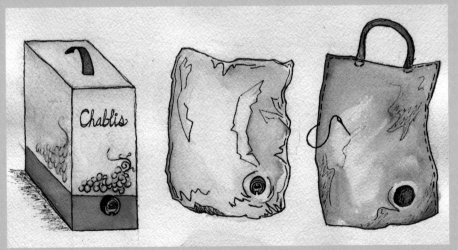

Make a featherweight water bag by removing the silver lining from a wine box and sewing a container for the bag from ripstop nylon. Leave the space between the hanging straps open to insert and remove the lining.
To fill with water, pry off plastic nozzle with the back or dull edge of your knife. The nozzle will snap back into place.

panion vial of tablets that are mixed with the iodine to make the water more palatable. Although iodine tablets are effective against *Giardia,* they don't remove some chemical and bacterial pollutants; iodine may also be unsafe for pregnant women or people who suffer from a thyroid condition. But iodine's convenience and light weight make it popular. Every backpacker should carry a vial of iodine tablets, just in case the stove gives out or a filter pump breaks.

Filter pumps are the most effective way to treat water. They remove most bacterial contaminants and can adequately purify almost any drinking source, including some of the suspect liquids adventurous hikers occasionally resort to, such as elk wallows or the green soup in a cattle tank. However, pumps are fragile, a bit on the bulky side, and the filters tend to clog up and need replacement before the manufacturer's claim for longevity has expired. Newer models are sturdier and more reliable, but you still must keep them from being squashed in your pack. Carry your filter inside a cookpot for safety.

BACKPACKING FOODS AND COOKERY

I once went backpacking with a woman who was a personal trainer in New York City. The first thing she did when we returned to civilization was stand on a bathroom scales.

"I don't believe it," she said. "You can eat all that you want, everything tastes great, and you still lose weight. If the women at the gym knew about this, I'd be out of a job."

The reason is simple mathematics: backpackers burn off more calories than they can comfortably carry in their packs. Nutritionists estimate that hikers need to consume from 3,000 to more than 5,000 calories each day to keep up their energy. That's about double the usual daily recommendation and most backpackers don't reach it. Losing a few pounds is okay as long as you limit your stay in the wilderness to a week or less. Long-distance hikers, however, need to be much more conscientious about their food intake (see Chapter 11).

Complex carbohydrates, which transfer sugar into the bloodstream at an even rate to provide a sustained release of energy, are the body's preferred source of fuel for endurance sports. They should constitute about 60 percent of your daily calories. Cereals, bagels, rice, pasta, and instant mashed potatoes are examples of backpacking fare that is rich in carbohydrates. Your diet should be low in protein (10 to 15 percent) and *relatively* low in fat (20 to 30 percent). However, it's important not to get rid of the fats altogether. They

How Much Food Do You Need?

Backpackers tend to take too much of everything, with the one exception of food. Even if you pack mostly dry-mix and freeze-dried meals, it takes a couple of pounds of food per day to stoke your furnace with the calories it needs. Read the labels carefully to make sure you will be getting adequate nutrition. And bring at least one extra day's food supply, in case you become injured or have to spend an extra night in the woods for some other reason.

have a very high calorie-to-weight ratio, which is crucial when you can carry only so much food. And fats metabolize slowly, continuing to boost your energy long after your body has burned off carbohydrates.

Good sources of fats include cheeses, peanut butter, margarine, butter, and chocolate. Jerky and nuts, along with small cans of meat to spice up dinners of rice and pasta, add the needed dash of protein.

Breakfast

Most backpackers like to keep breakfasts simple, in order to hit the trail early. A granola bar and a few swallows of water, or a bowl of whole-grain cereals, such as granola or Muesli, mixed with water and dried milk, offer a quick and nutritious breakfast. Flake cereals tend to become ground into powder from jostling in the food bag and are better left at home. Instant oatmeal or Cream of Wheat packets provide a hot breakfast, but allow at least two packets per day at the minimum. Many hikers also enjoy a cup of hot soup or ramen noodles for breakfast. If you are on a weekend outing where weight doesn't matter so much, a fresh bagel or slice of banana bread with cream cheese offers a tasty breakfast treat.

Hot beverages are a personal choice, although too much caffeinated coffee can act as a diuretic, setting the stage for dehydration down the trail. If you are a coffee drinker, coffee bags offer a better grade of java than instant for a few more pennies.

Lunch

Backpackers seldom stick to strict lunch hours, or, for that matter, to traditional lunch foods such as sandwiches and fresh fruit. Because a working body needs constant restoking, it's healthier to munch on dried fruits, peanuts, jerky, trail mixes, and trail bars during each rest stop, saving your one big meal for dinner.

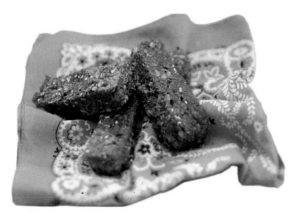

Trail snacks eaten at frequent intervals are high in carbohydrates and help provide the sustained release of energy needed for hiking.

Other lunch possibilities include cheeses and hard salami, which keep better than you would expect in all but the hottest weather. They provide the fat content needed during heavy exertion, particularly in cold weather.

Use small-size margarine tubs to keep fragile foods like crackers or a piece of pie (a great treat your first day out) from being squished in the food bag.

Dinner

Backpacking dinners need to be portable—lightweight, compact, and possessing a relatively long shelf life. And meals should cook quickly, to conserve on fuel.

Today's freeze-dried meals fill the bill perfectly and are quite delicious. (First-generation meals, on the other hand, tasted like cardboard or worse.) Equally as important, many freeze-dried entrees need no more than the addition of boiled water to the foil package. The drawbacks are the price and quantity of food. Backpackers are gourmands, not gourmets, and a dinner that advertises for two to three people is probably just about right for one. Veteran hikers learn to stretch freeze-dried meals by having a first course of ramen noodles or Cup-A-Soup to take the edge off the hunger before the main course is served.

Other dinner standbys include macaroni and cheese, boxed rice and pasta dishes, instant mashed potatoes, couscous, and stuffing mixes. Just be sure to read the cooking instructions before making your purchases, and choose mixes that need only a few minutes cooking time. Discard boxes and repackage all the mixes in reclosable, heavy-duty freezer bags. Add a can of turkey or beef and you have the equivalent of a freeze-dried dinner, for only a couple ounces more and about half the price.

Don't forget to pack a few squares of aluminum foil for cooking trout from an alpine lake. Most high altitude waters in backpacking meccas are naturally

Fresh-caught trout from a lake in the high Sierras—a delight to tastebuds numbed by days of freeze-dried meals.

sterile, with no adequate spawning gravel where wild trout can reproduce. Fish are stocked periodically and killing a few small ones (check regulations first) does little harm to these fisheries. Brook trout, in particular, tend to overpopulate and stunt. You'll be doing their brothers a favor by taking a few on a fly, not to mention delighting tastebuds dulled by days of trail food. Just add a tablespoon of oil to the lid of your cookpot, sprinkle the fish with salt and pepper, and fry them crisp. You can eat the trout heads, tails, and all.

Keep It Simple, Keep It Clean

"Simplify, simplify," wrote Henry David Thoreau. Nowhere is his dictum more relevant than in backpack cooking. Stick to one-pot meals and use the bag the meal came in or a heavy, reclosable freezer bag for the cooking. Just add hot water to the bag and immerse it into more hot water inside the pot. That way you don't have to clean the pot, and dishwashing is reduced to a quick rinse of a cup and spoon.

Spicing It Up

Almost any rice or pasta dish can be made better by the addition of herbs such as thyme and oregano, which you can keep pre-mixed in a small plastic bag with a twist tie. Try a pinch of garlic powder for spicing up instant mashed potatoes, or a sprinkling of

Parmesan cheese, which enlivens almost any dish. A small vial of soy sauce, some dried gourmet mushrooms, or a packet of powdered sauce mix are other options—experiment and let your imagination be your guide. Don't forget a handful of chicken and beef boullion cubes or a packet of miso, an Asian specialty, to flavor bland dishes.

Mustard keeps longer than mayonnaise and adds pizzazz to hard salami or pepperoni sticks. Clarified butter keeps well and adds needed fat to your diet.

THE ETHICS OF FIRE

In no other area are the principles of no-trace camping more hotly debated than the practice of fire building. Fire can be a wonderful tonic to a weary backpacker at day's end, offering light, warmth, and security during the hours when human courage reaches its lowest ebb. A campfire can serve as a catalyst that draws words from the heart and wonder from the soul. But in many areas the wood we gather for fire robs the forest floor of nutrients provided by decomposition. Fire also sterilizes the organic soil that is the lifeblood of plant life and it scars the earth, reminding us that no matter how far we may have walked, others have left their marks before us.

In many national parks and in some wilderness areas, backcountry fires are strictly prohibited. On other public lands they are generally permitted, although seasonal restrictions may apply during the dry days of late summer.

Should you build a fire? No, at least not in meadows, above tree line, or in other fragile ecosystems. In fact, many backpackers discourage fire building anywhere.

However, in forests where fire danger is low, it is possible to build a *minimum-impact* fire that leaves no sign of your passing. There are two ways of doing this. The first is the pit fire, built in a trench dug in the earth. Choose sand or pebbly mineral soil for the pit. Do not make a pit fire in loamy organic earth. Dig a hole a foot or a little more in circumference and at least 8 inches deep. Keep your fire small and use only dead wood found on the ground. In the morning, scoop the earth you had removed back into the hole and litter twigs and leaves over the top to blend in with the adjoining ground cover.

The second method, which is less damaging to the environment, is to make a mound of mineral soil several inches deep and build the fire on top. Look for mineral soil near stream beds and in the cavities of uprooted stumps. In the morning, scatter the ashes and return the mineral soil to the site where you had found it. To make returning the soil simple, place a ground cloth or a sheet of thin metal (they are sold in some outdoor outfitters, or you can

Fire is the magic candle of wilderness—a hearth away from home for a weary backpacker. But be aware that fire-building can damage fragile environments.

create a makeshift one from tin sheeting) on the ground before heaping the mineral soil on top. Then just lift up the pan or gather the edges of the cloth and haul the soil away.

THE BACKCOUNTRY LATRINE

Entire books have been written on this subject, some with amusingly descriptive titles and rolls of toilet paper pictured on the covers. But disposing of human wastes in an environmentally friendly manner can easily be summed up in a few sentences.

When you need to urinate, walk at least 200 feet from camp or any water source and direct your urine flow directly onto the ground; its chemical composition is nearly sterile and will do no damage to plants or soil. For feces disposal, pack a small plastic toilet trowel. Walk 200 feet or more from any water source, dig a cat hole about six inches deep, do your business, and cover it up with soil. Feces decompose quickly in rich, damp organic soil, so choose that type for your cat hole rather than sand or mineral soil. In remote areas, some backpackers advocate defecating on top of a rock, then smearing the feces with a stick to expose more surface area to the air. The smeared feces will decompose much more quickly than feces buried in the ground.

Toilet paper, along with any other paper garbage, should either be *completely burned* in a hot fire or, preferably, packed out in a plastic sack. Many backpackers simplify their lives by dispensing with toilet paper and using natural materials for wiping, such as leaves (not poison ivy!), barkless sticks, smooth stones, or snow.

In fragile areas that see a lot of human traffic, specifically river canyon corridors where travel is confined to the banks, human feces can contaminate the water and should be packed out. Double-sack them, using opaque plastic bags, and wrap securely to prevent odors from leaking. Do the same with women's tampons.

A FINAL THOUGHT

I realize that some prospective backpackers may finish this chapter with a skeptical smile. Sure, they say to themselves, respecting the land is an admirable attribute, but aren't some of the measures recommended here a little Draconian? Is it really necessary to erase every evidence of our fires or pack out garbage when it could be buried out of sight? And

Tips for No-Trace Camping

In addition to following guidelines for human waste disposal and choosing environmentally friendly campsites, bear these tips in mind for keeping your impact on the environment to a minimum.

• Stay on trails. Do not take shortcuts where trails switchback on steep grades. Bushwhacking in sensitive areas damages vegetation and causes erosion.

• Keep your party size small. If you are backpacking in a group of eight or more, break up into smaller parties.

• Choose neutral colors for tents, backpacks, and other gear that announces human presence. It makes the backcountry appear less crowded.

• Never bury garbage. Pack it out in plastic bags to minimize odor.

• Do not wash yourself, your clothing, or your dinner dishes directly in a water source. Instead, carry water away from the source and use as little as possible for washing up.

• Even biodegradable soap is too harsh on fragile environments. Make do with water for all washing needs; heat it if necessary.

• Don lightweight camp shoes around the tent site. Aqua socks and amphibious (Teva-type) sports sandals are the best choices, doubling as wading shoes at river crossings. They do less damage to vegetation than boots.

• After packing up in the morning, take time to fluff up trampled vegetation and return the area to its natural-looking state.

A pair of elk in a spring meadow.

what's wrong with hiking off-trail through a meadow for a closer look at a band of elk? The truth is, nothing would be wrong with these practices if we were the only humans using the country. But we aren't. More than 15 million Americans backpack each year and the number of visitors in wilderness areas alone has grown by more than 400 percent since 1965. Although it is still possible to find places where you can travel without seeing evidence of another human visitor, many areas have become so overcrowded that one must apply for a permit.

Backpacking is a privilege, not a right. Our freedom to wander depends upon the land's ability to withstand our impact. By taking steps to minimize that impact, we not only honor the land but preserve the heritage of backpacking for our children and grandchildren.

CHAPTER
9

Creature Discomforts

"Where they set their paws the magnetic alignment of the earth is disturbed, so that a visitor feels both the attraction and repulsion of tumbling poles. It draws him around the bend and scares him at the same time. Perhaps we all seek places where air is soured by bears and trees grow too close together."

KEITH MCCAFFERTY

Hikers and backpackers are drawn to wilderness to see wildlife. Most of the time, we don't see enough of it. But once in a while, we come across the wrong animal in the wrong place, at the wrong time.

In a lifetime of wandering, I have been growled at by mountain lions, bluff-charged by a grizzly bear, and have mimicked the silent horror of Edvard Munch's famous painting, "The Scream," after being attacked by insects that inflicted misery out of all proportion to their size. With a little forethought and a few ounces of aerosol prevention, the itching, injury, and sheer terror that resulted from those confrontations could have been tempered or avoided altogether.

BEARS, LIONS, AND OTHER PREDATORS

Safety in Bear Country

Bear confrontations along the trail are almost always a result of hikers approaching too closely, before the bear becomes aware of their presence. Most bears run when being startled at close range. But a few are provoked into a

129

You can't outswim him; you can't outrun him. Give grizzly bears the respect—and space—they deserve. This is way too close for comfort.

territorial response, consisting of growling, snapping teeth, bluff charges, and in a few cases outright attack. The formidable grizzly bear of the Rocky Mountain West is more protective of its territory than its smaller cousin, the black bear, and more likely to press an attack. Sows with cubs are the most dangerous bears; if you can see them clearly without binoculars, you are probably too close for safety.

To avoid encounters, stick to major trails and talk loudly when passing through dense cover. If you encounter an aggressive bear, resist the urge to run, which can trigger an attack. Stand as a group and talk softly to the bear. Back away slowly. Avoid direct eye contact, which the bear can interpret as aggressive behavior. If a bear pursues, drop an item from your pack (not food!) to distract its attention. If you can climb a tree, by all means do so.

And if the bear charges? The rule of thumb with grizzlies is drop to the ground, curl into a fetal position, and place your hands over your head for protection. Most grizzlies are content to bat you around until they sense the danger is gone. Blacks that press an attack may not be so easily mollified. Some experts believe you should fight back at blacks with anything you can grab, such as a big stick.

Many backpackers carry cayenne pepper aerosol sprays, which have been proven to deter determined charges by bears—*in most cases*. If you decide to carry pepper spray, keep it in a belt holster (sold with the can of some brands); people who have been attacked almost invariably report that the

Mountain lion tracks in New Mexico's Sangre De Cristo Mountains: a not-so-subtle reminder that in some places man is not always at the top of the food chain.

The best way to keep bears from associating food with humans is to hang food, cookstove, toothbrush, and any other scented items in a tree.
1. *Walk a couple hundred feet downwind of your camp. Select a tree that has a stout branch growing at right angles about 20 feet off the ground.*
2. *Tie a rock to one end of a 50-foot length of nylon cord and toss it over the branch, at least 10 feet out from the trunk.*
3. *Tie food bag to one end of the rope and pull the bag high under the branch.*
4. *Tie counterweight (another food bag or a rock) to the rope as high as you can reach, winding up excess rope and leaving loops for retrieval.*
5. *Push second bag up with a stick until both bags are balanced at least 10 feet in the air. Use the stick to catch a loop of rope and pull it down in the morning.*

charge was instantaneous, so you will have no time to zip open a compartment in your pack. Get a 12-ounce canister and make sure the contents contain no less 10 percent oleoresin capsicum. Test-spray it once to become familiar with its operation. Don't become overconfident. A calm head and caution are still the best protection you can take into bear country.

A bear that attacks human beings in their tents at night will not be content to stop after a few paw swipes. Fight

Fishing in Bear Country

Disposing of fish guts in most areas means burying them away from the water's edge, where they can decompose and enrich the soil. But in bear country, it's best to throw heads, tails, and innards as far as you can into a deep part of the lake, where the bruin's sensitive nose will not be so easily alerted.

back with anything you can. Many backpackers pitch their tents near a climbable tree in grizzly country. I'm one of them.

Mountain Lions

An upsurge in deer populations and the growing number of hikers and backpackers in western states have resulted in an increase in mountain lion/human confrontations, a handful of which have ended in tragedy.

Most lions that attack humans are young animals driven to the fringes of civilization by larger, territorial males. Most documented attacks recorded have targeted women and children.

When hiking in lion country, keep the smaller members of your party between the larger adults. Most big cats are reluctant to attack people head-on, so in a confrontation, face the lion, make yourself appear as large as possible, and use any means to fight back and discourage the attack. I was once stalked by a pair of young lions while hiking in Montana's Gallatin Range. It was night, and each time one turned to face the beam of my headlamp, its eyes glowed like jade fire. The pair of lions growled continuously and followed me to the bank of the river, where they sat like bookends and stared with those green eyes as I waded across. Luckily, they did not push an attack. The lesson to be learned from that incident is that the odds of crossing paths with a predator are higher at night, when they are actively hunting.

But my experience remains rare. While hiking and backpacking, you are far more likely to be struck by lightning than by fang or claw.

Mountain lion attacks are rare, but growing populations of both hikers and cats have resulted in many confrontations over the past decade. Keep children close when traveling through brushy areas of the West.

Two-Legged Predators

Crime is not a major concern in the backcountry and the farther you travel from major cities and developed roads, the less you have to worry about. Unfortunately, we live in a world where no place is truly safe. Lone hikers, particularly women, are most at risk. The best way to avoid problems is to hike in parties and camp well away from anyone who appears sullen, overly friendly, or suspicious. Leave a detailed itinerary at home and don't broadcast to strangers where you plan to camp.

Vandalism is not unheard of on wilderness trails, but the bigger problem is at trailheads where hikers leave their cars. In some parts of the East, particularly near the Appalachian Trail, car vandalism is enough of a problem that smart hikers arrange to leave their vehicles in motel parking lots or even along residential streets, then hitch a ride to the trailhead. You can contact the Appalachian Trail Conference (see References) for a list of people who will shuttle you to the trailhead or drive your car to a safe parking area farther down the trail.

BITERS, STINGERS, AND BLOOD-SUCKING PESTS

Biting Insects

Mosquitoes, along with their pinpoint cousins, black flies and no-see-ums, have probably ruined more backpacking trips than anything but pouring rain. The first line of defense against these aerial warriors is timing. If possible, avoid the peak breeding season in early summer. Problems diminish later on, when the female mosquito is no longer looking for blood to nourish her eggs and the onset of short days and crisp nights drops a blanket over insect activity.

In buggy areas, wear loose-fitting, tightly woven clothing and use rubber bands on your cuffs. The most effective insect repellent is DEET, a chemical compound that confuses the insects' sensors, causing them to stay in a holding pattern rather than land and bite. However, exposure to DEET has been known to cause harmful side effects, including rashes, eye and sinus problems, headaches, and insomnia. Adults should use a 30- to 35-percent solution, children a 10-percent solution. Kids less than two years old should not be exposed to DEET.

Natrapel, Avon's Skin-So-Soft, and other products containing *citronella,* a plant derivative, repel mosquitoes and black flies less effectively than DEET and must be applied more often. However, citronella has no side effects and most hikers build up a partial immunity to insect bites, rendering DEET unnecessary after the first few days.

In severely infested areas, you can spray your clothing and tent screening with *permethrin,* sold under several trade names as a tick repellent. It is an insecticide that kills bugs on contact, but is not harmful to humans.

Larger biting insects, including horseflies, deer flies, and stable flies, are only somewhat deterred by repellents. They are attracted to food and bright colors, so keep food put away and dress in muted tones. Pick camping spots that are exposed to evening breezes.

Treatment

Calamine lotion and over-the-counter steroid creams will dull the itch of insect bites. More powerful prescription steroids are available from your doctor. Oral antihistamines also help.

Stinging Insects

Bees, wasps, and hornets seldom present much of a problem on hiking trails. But do keep in mind that bees are irritable on overcast days and can be attracted to blue and yellow clothing. Avoid hornet nests and beehives, and keep a good distance from a swarm of bees that are flying in a straight line. They are likely returning to a hive and will be aggressive.

Food-loving yellow jackets can be bothersome in some camping sites. Setting a piece of meat or a cup of a sugary sports drink to one side of your campsite may keep the yellow jackets occupied long enough for you to eat dinner.

Treatment

To remove a stinger, scrape it with the back of a knife blade. Be careful not to squeeze the stinger and release more venom. The ointments and oral antihistamines used to treat mosquito bites can help with the stinging.

Allergic reactions to bee, wasp, hornet, and yellow jacket stings claim more than 100 lives a year in our country. People who are allergic should never hike without a beesting kit that includes an epinephrine self-injector, which causes clogged airways to expand and keeps the heartbeat regular until the beesting victim can reach a hospital.

Ticks

The deer tick that transmits Lyme disease is very common in some parts of the Eastern Seaboard region, where the ticks feed on the blood of their namesake host, the whitetail deer. But deer and other disease-carrying ticks are widespread in the Midwest and West, too. To avoid ticks, stick to the trail and don't walk through tall grasses. Wear long-sleeved shirts and long pants (put rubber bands on the cuffs) in light colors, so that you can spot any tick that clings to the fabric. Re-

Deer tick (oversize). In early summer, the deer tick is about the size of a letter on this page.

member that some ticks are no larger than a period on this sheet of paper. Check your body and your hairline for ticks at least twice a day.

Treatment

To remove a tick, grasp it with tweezers close to the skin and pull the tick straight out. Don't crush the body, which increases the chance of infection. And make sure you get all the head and mouth parts out of your skin.

Most people who contract Lyme disease develop a bull's-eye-like rash at the site of the bite within 3 to 30 days after being infected. Symptoms include fatigue, fever, and headache. Pinpoint-sized blood spots on the wrists, ankles, the palms of the hands or the soles of the feet, accompanied by fever and chills, are early warnings of Rocky Mountain spotted fever, another tick-related disease. Both can be cured by antibiotics, but arthritis, heart, and neurological problems can result for those who go untreated.

Spiders and Scorpions

The female black widow spider is a round-bodied, shiny black spider with an orange or red hourglass on her abdomen (see illustration). Brown recluse spiders are light-colored with brown, violin-shaped markings on their backs (see illustration on next page). Both of these large spiders are widespread, although the brown recluse spins its web mainly south

Black widow spider (female)

Brown recluse spider

of the Mason-Dixon line. Both species can inflect serious bites that warrant medical attention.

The stings of most scorpion species are neither dangerous nor particularly painful. However, the bark scorpion of the Sonoran Desert, which is yellowish brown with dark stripes down its back and has a nasty-looking knob at the base of its stinger, can inject a neurotoxic venom similar to that of cobras (albeit in a much smaller dose). Hikers should take precautions such as shaking out their boots and socks before dressing each morning. Do not carelessly poke under logs and stones with your fingers.

Treatment

The bite of the black widow is initially painless, but sweating and cramping of the muscles near the site of the bite typically follow within an hour. The bite of the brown recluse spider is extremely painful and is rapidly followed by severe swelling. Swallow aspirin and hike purposefully but without panic to the nearest trailhead, flag a car, and get to a hospital.

The pain from the sting of the bark scorpion usually fades away in a couple of hours. But children and the elderly, or anyone who has high blood pressure, may experience tingling, rapid pulse, soaring blood pressure, or difficulty in breathing. Seek medical attention as soon as possible.

Poisonous Snakes

None of the four varieties of American poisonous snakes are overtly aggressive and they are all easily identified (see illustrations) and avoided. Copperheads are an eastern snake, commonly found in fields, hardwood forests, and among stone ledges. Water moccasins are larger (up to 4½ feet long) and much heavier-bodied. These snakes, also known as "cottonmouths," frequent swampy lowlands in the Southeast and can appear almost black when they are wet from swimming. Rattlesnakes are distinguished by their prominent heads and the segmented rattle at the base of their tails. They range in size from the diminutive but pugnacious pygmy rattlesnake, which seldom exceeds 15 inches in length, to the massive eastern diamondback rattlesnake of the Southeast, which can reach a length of 7 feet. Coral snakes are small,

Copperhead

Western diamondback rattlesnake

Coral snake

Water moccasin (Cottonmouth)

southern reptiles; they are related to cobras and their venom is equally toxic. However, coral snakes seldom bite unless roughly handled.

Hikers and backpackers can minimize the chances of contact with poisonous snakes by sticking to open trails, by checking with a flashlight before walking around at night, especially in hot weather, and by looking first before they haul themselves up step inclines by holding onto rock ledges.

Treatment

The best first aid for snakebite is a set of car keys to get the victim to the hospital. If you are bitten, keep the wounded limb below heart level and walk to the nearest road. There's no need to panic. Unless you were struck by a large specimen of the eastern or western diamondback, or by the desert-dwelling

Mojave rattler, your chance of dying is remote. If you are planning on a trip in an area known to have many poisonous snakes, such as the Grand Canyon in Arizona, it might be a good idea to purchase a Sawyer Extractor, which, if promptly applied, can suction much of the venom from the wound site, minimizing tissue destruction.

POISONOUS PLANTS

For people who are sensitive to *urushiol*, the chemical compound found in the leaves, stems, and roots of poison ivy, poison oak, and poison sumac, a hiking trip in almost any corner of the United States can result in a souvenir rash that itches for days.

Learn to identify these plants before you go hiking (see illustration). Both poison ivy and its western cousin, poison oak, can grow as ground cover, trailing shrubs, or rope-like, woody vines. Poison sumac is a tall, swamp-loving, rangy shrub with between 7 and 13 smooth-edged leaflets per stem.

There are places in New England where it is impossible to avoid contact with poison ivy, and I have hiked in areas near the California coast where blankets of poison oak made bushwhacking almost suicidal.

Avoid problems by sticking to the trail. Remember, too, that the oil from these plants will rub off on your hiking stick or the coat of a dog. My wife once contracted a horrible rash of poison oak on her feet when urushiol vapor permeated the socks she was drying over a backcountry campfire in California's Sequoia Park. No doubt a stem of poison oak had been inadvertently tossed into the flames.

Poison ivy (bottom). Poison oak (top).

The Mud-Pack Cure

Barrier lotions that prevent urushiol from penetrating the skin are a godsend for hikers who venture into poison ivy- or poison oak-infested forests. These lotions are sold in outdoor stores and drugstores under trade names such as Ivy Block, Ivy Shield, and Stokogard Outdoor Cream. The lotion dries into a clay-like coating. It must be reapplied every four hours to ensure protection, but anyone who has had a bad case of the itch will assure you that the alternative can be much, much worse.

Treatment

Once urushiol gets on your skin, only prompt washing with water can prevent the rash. Rinse skin and clothing that might have touched the plant and hope for the best.

Redness and swelling usually occur a day or two after initial contact. The watery blisters that erupt in severe cases don't contain urushiol and are not contagious. Although the rash is very unpleasant, it usually subsides within a couple of weeks.

Cortisone shots and oral corticosteroids (available by prescription) offer the only truly effective treatment and work best if taken at the first indication of a rash. Topical steroid creams, such as Cortaid and Lanacort, offer temporary relief, as do antihistamines and oatmeal baths.

Boardwalks like this one can keep you from tromping through poisonous plants, which often grow at the edge of the trail.

CHAPTER
10

Injury and Illness

"Walking is man's best medicine."

HIPPOCRATES

A s the Health and Safety columnist for *Field&Stream,* I have spoken with many hikers, hunters, and fishermen who have been injured or fallen sick in the wilderness. With the exception of outfitters and guides, who must complete a course in wilderness medicine before they can be licensed, few of the victims had taken precautions against mishaps or knew the correct first aid treatment.

If you are planning to spend much time outdoors, sign up for a course in wilderness medicine. Courses are offered by private companies such as the Wilderness Medical Training Center, which often contract through colleges and universities. See the Reference section at the back of this book for more information. Your knowledge could comfort a companion or save a life.

HYPOTHERMIA

Near my home in Montana, a hiker dies from hypothermia nearly every other year, sometimes in the middle of summer when daytime temperatures climb into the 80's. As long as it gets cool in the evening, any number of variables, such as becoming wet with perspiration or from a fall into a creek, being chilled by wind, or being unable to move due to injury, can combine to put hikers at risk. In fact, many of the states with the highest rate of hypothermia are in the South—places that have rapidly changing temperatures from shifting weather systems, such as Virginia and the Carolinas, or high elevation

High altitude, chill winds, storm clouds brewing. This is hypothermia country. Clothing that retains body heat when wet and wicks moisture away from the skin is vital to your survival.

plateaus in New Mexico and Arizona, where temperatures plummet rapidly after sunset.

Early warnings of hypothermia include shivering, slurred speech, and loss of coordination. Keep an eye out for someone in your party with the "umbles"—hypothermia is characterized by stumbling, mumbling, fumbling, and bumbling. Pay particular attention to children, the elderly, or anyone who suffers from a chronic illness; they are more susceptible to hypothermia than healthy adults and may be less likely to communicate their discomfort.

Treatment

If someone in your party exhibits the symptoms of hypothermia, get him or her out of the wind, peel off any damp clothing, and warm up the victim with dry clothes or your own body heat. Place hot water bottles or rocks warmed in a fire (insulate them with cloth to avoid burns) against the victim's trunk, not against the arms or legs. Better yet, get the victim into a sleeping bag between two rescuers who can share body heat by pressing their torsos against the victim's chest and upper back. Encourage the victim to drink warm fluids.

A person whose core body temperature has plummeted below 90° F. will have stopped shivering, be unable to walk a straight line or follow other commands, may complain of poor vision, and may even begin to shed his clothing. The victim will breathe slowly and have poor reflexes. Do not massage the victim's arms or legs, because it can return cold, acidic blood to the body core and result in a shock to the system. Walking also pulses cold blood from the extremities into the chest cavity, so do not help the victim get up or permit him or her to walk until the arms and legs have been rewarmed through the normal circulation from body heat. Victims of severe hypothermia are at risk of ventricular fibrillation, the chaotic quivering of the heart that can result in death. There are records of hypothermia victims who have dropped dead from fibrillation when they began walking after being rescued, presumably because cold blood from the arms and legs circulated through the heart.

Because it is difficult to determine how far hypothermia has progressed without a hypothermia thermometer, stay on the safe side and treat all victims very gently.

ALTITUDE SICKNESS

Altitude sickness is brought about by the lower concentration of oxygen at high altitudes. It is sometimes referred to as "drunkard's syndrome," because as the saturation of oxygen in the blood falls, the victim undergoes mood changes such as lassitude and becomes unable to think clearly or walk in a straight line. Other symptoms are nausea, headache, dizziness, fitful sleep, shortness of breath, and dry cough.

About one of every four hikers who live at sea level will fall victim to acute mountain sickness (AMS), the most common form of altitude sickness, if they climb rapidly to 7,000 feet; about half will become ill at 10,000 feet. A person's susceptibility has little to do with his age, sex, or even his physical fitness.

Acclimation is the key to avoiding problems. If you have flown from sea level to high altitude, rest in town overnight before driving or hiking higher. As a rule of thumb, climb no more than 2,000 feet a day at altitudes above 6,000 feet, and drop back down if you start to feel dizzy or nauseated. People who suffer from altitude sickness often want to be left alone. Do not grant their wishes. Always hike in parties at high altitude. Keep in mind that hikers who climb several hundred feet higher than their camp and return to lower elevation to sleep are less likely to become impaired with AMS than those who camp at the highest altitude they reached that day.

Treatment

Aspirin or acetaminophen will help relieve headaches associated with AMS. Most symptoms of mild altitude sickness will resolve in a couple of days. Those who begin to stagger, refuse to eat or drink, or who act irrationally should be immediately evacuated to a lower elevation. Supplemental oxygen is helpful and should be carried on organized expeditions to high altitudes.

LIGHTNING

Lightning poses one of the greatest dangers for hikers who climb above timberline. Never try to second-guess your safety by counting seconds between lightning strikes and peals of thunder. If the sky looks threatening, discard metal objects, such as external-frame packs, and seek shelter among bushes or rocks of uniform size. Stay off ridgelines and away from tall, tapering trees. Don't huddle in a damp depression; a low damp spot can conduct ground electricity from a strike that may be hundreds of feet away. Squat with your feet together or sit on a foam sleeping pad or other non-conductive material to insulate your body from ground shock.

Lightning can zap the human body with 100 million volts of electricity. Timberline in Yosemite is no place to be in a storm. Seek shelter among smaller trees and separate so that if one in your party is struck, others can begin CPR.

If you are hiking in a group, split up, but don't separate so far from each other that you lose eye contact. That way, if one person or group is hit, members of the other group can begin to administer first aid.

Treatment

The immediate concern in a lightning strike is that the electrical charge, which can galvanize the human body with 100 million volts of electricity, will shock the respiratory and cardiac system, leading to respiratory and cardiac arrest. In cases of lightning strike, attend to those who appear dead first. Promptly administer rescue breathing if the victim is not breathing, but has a pulse. If you cannot find a pulse and the victim is not breathing, administer full cardiopulmonary resuscitation (CPR). Do not be discouraged by the ashen visage of the victim. A hiker in Yellowstone National Park who was struck by lightning showed no sign of life for an hour during CPR efforts, before she finally began to breathe on her own. Send a member of your party for medical help and don't give up until it arrives.

BURNS

Burns can be caused by careless handling of backpacking stoves and candle lanterns, by tripping and falling into campfires, and by campfire sparks that result in corneal burns of the eye. Other burns result from steam or hot water spilled when someone picks up a cooking pot by a hot handle and reflexively drops it.

I once attempted to remove the butane canister from a backpacking stove before it was entirely empty. It shot out a jet of fuel, which caught fire from a nearby candle. Fortunately, I had the presence of mind to kick the canister upright, where it shot flames 10 feet into the air like a Roman candle before the fuel ran out.

"That's what Hemingway called 'grace under pressure,' " I said to my backpacking companion when the flame died away. She was not amused.

Treatment

Anyone whose clothing has caught fire must immediately *stop, drop,* and *roll.* Smother flames with jackets or a sleeping bag and quickly remove wristwatches, jewelry, or any burned clothing that can retain heat (polypropylene and fleece are notorious in this respect). Reduce the temperature of skin burns with cool water, either by immersing the limb or applying wet cloth.

But be careful—too much evaporative cooling can make the victim hypothermic. Clean the wound with disinfected or boiled, cooled water and dress the burn with an antiseptic ointment or cream such as silver sulfadiazine (Silvadene), which you should have in your medical kit. Wrap the burned area with a clean bandage (sterile gauze, if possible, or in an emergency, a clean T-shirt). If it will take several days to hike to a road, remove the dressing, clean the skin carefully, and reapply a dressing once a day. Ibuprofen can help ease the pain.

Burns often are much more serious than they initially appear to be. Full-thickness burns that go deeper than the dermis layer of the skin may not hurt because the blood vessels and nerve endings have been destroyed. If you have any doubt about the severity, keep the bandage in place, hike to the nearest road and flag down a ride to an emergency room.

SUNBURN

The first line of defense against sunburn is protective clothing. Wear loose-fitting pants and long-sleeved shirts in light colors. Dense weaves block UV radiation best; the labels of some tropical nylon and polyester clothing tout that it promotes evaporative cooling while blocking all the sun's harmful radiation. Don't forget a broad-brimmed hat with a flap on the sides and back to protect your neck and ears.

Apply sunscreen with an SPF rating of at least 15 to *all* exposed skin an hour or so before exposure, preferably onto cool, dry skin. Hiking generates a lot of sweat. For most sunscreens to remain effective, you will have to reapply them every couple of hours. Hikers who have fair skin or spend many hours in direct sunlight should consider using physical sunblocks on the nose, ears, cheeks, and lips; opaque pastes such as zinc oxide block transmission of all solar radiation.

Try also to limit your exposure as much as possible during the hours of the sun's greatest intensity, usually between 9 A.M. and 3 P.M.

Treatment

Cool, wet compresses offer a temporary respite from sunburn pain. Topical anesthetic sprays may cause an allergic reaction and should be used with caution. Mentholated lotions and aloe vera jells provide some relief, as do anti-inflammatories such as ibuprofen. Topical steroid creams can help ease pain, but should not be applied over blistered skin. My brother, who is an emergency physician, has had the best results by treating sunburned hikers with a prescription-strength lotion that contains an anti-inflammatory. Severe cases of sunburn should be treated by a physician.

HEAT-RELATED ILLNESSES

Heat exhaustion is the most common form of heat illness. It tends to afflict hikers who are not acclimated to high heat and humidity and have neglected to replenish electrolytes and water lost through their exertions. Symptoms include nausea, headache, weakness, confusion, chills, faintness, and rapid pulse. Victims often have cool, clammy skin.

To stave off heat exhaustion, limit your exposure during the heat of the day and drink lots of fluids to replace salts lost through sweating. Rest often, and if you must hike during midday, periodically dip your handkerchief or hat into water to get some evaporative cooling underway as you walk.

Heat stroke is a true medical emergency. Disorientation, loss of coordination, and stroke-like symptoms, such as weakness or numbness on one side of the body, are typical. Elderly victims may be hot and dry to the touch, because their sweating function is less functional than the younger or physically-fit, who may continue to sweat. Unlike heat exhaustion, which typically does not raise the victim's core body temperature to a dangerous level, heat-stroke victims have soaring temperatures. Only prompt action can prevent death.

Treatment

Victims of heat exhaustion will recover if you get them out of the sun and have them drink lots of fluids. Water is fine, but a half-and-half mix of water and a sports drink such as Gatorade is better, because it replaces more of the electrolytes lost through sweating. If you suspect a hiking companion is suffering from heat stroke, strip his or her clothes off at once. Cool the victim's body by rubbing the skin down with a wet cloth, then remove the fabric to al-

Teach Your Body How to Sweat

Acclimization is a big factor in heat-related illnesses. The body's sweating mechanism needs to adjust to strenuous activity in hot climates. Until the body learns to produce more sweat at a lower temperature, the core temperature climbs too high and heat exhaustion or heat stroke can result. Start teaching your body how to sweat at home by engaging in vigorous activity in the heat for an hour or so a day for a few weeks prior to the trip.

low evaporative cooling. Fanning the victim or opening the car window to allow a breeze will aid the cooling process. When the body temperature begins to decline and the victim is rational, encourage him or her to drink lots of fluids. *Do not have the victim swallow aspirin or acetaminophen.* If you are lucky enough to have an ice chest back in your car, place ice packs or cold beverage cans in the victim's armpits, groin area, and on the neck. Get the victim to a hospital as quickly as possible.

DEHYDRATION

An adult hiker needs lots of water, at least two liters of water a day, and much more in hot weather and at high altitudes. A good gauge of adequate hydration is urine color. Dark yellow or orange urine may indicate dehydration. If your urine isn't clear and copious, you probably aren't drinking enough water.

Treatment

Sports drinks such as Gatorade help replace salt and other electrolytes lost during sweating. But pure water is important, too, especially for waste elimination. For this reason, some experts recommend diluting sports-drink mixes to half strength with water. If you don't pack a sports-drink mix, you can replenish your body with electrolytes by adding to one quart or liter of drinking water the following ingredients: ¾ tsp. salt, ½ tsp. baking soda, ¼ tsp. potassium chloride (salt substitute), and 6 tsp. sugar.

GIARDIA

Giardia lamblia is a microscopic protozoan cyst deposited into water sources along with the feces of animals. With the exception of springs issuing from the earth, no water is safe from *Giardia;* backpackers have even contracted giardiasis from glacier melt. Disinfect all water either by boiling, adding iodine, or filtering it with a pump (see Chapter 8 for a more detailed discussion of water disinfection).

Treatment

Medical treatment to cure giardiasis is straightforward and effective, but the infection can be difficult to diagnose because the cyst has a long incubation time (from a few days to several weeks) and does not always show up in a stool sample. Stomach cramps, flatulence, and diarrhea are the obvious indicators, but they are not always present. After a camping trip, my brother's son lost weight steadily over a period of six months. He underwent a battery of medical tests before the doctors finally suspected *Giardia*. So if you begin to suffer from weight loss, general malaise, or any type of intestinal illness in the wake of a backpacking trip, suspect a waterborne illness sooner rather than later.

ALLERGIES

With the exceptions of rain and mosquitoes, probably nothing causes so much misery for people who enjoy hiking and backpacking as allergies to windblown pollen. Many allergy sufferers believe that there is little they can do but bear the burden of runny noses, itching eyes, and incessant sneezing if they travel outdoors during the spring and summer, when pollen counts are highest; others simply wonder why their colds won't go away. Anyone who experiences the symptoms of seasonal allergies should visit an allergist, who can perform simple, painless skin tests to determine exactly which pollens each person is allergic to. Only by knowing the enemy can you effectively fight against him.

Avoidance and Treatment

The pollinating seasons for most species of trees, weeds, and grasses that can cause allergic reactions begin later the farther north you travel. An allergy sufferer who plans his or her outings to avoid the worst of the season, and who keeps in mind that pollen counts are highest during the mornings and on warm, dry, breezy days, and lowest in the afternoons and during damp, chilly weather, may be able to circumvent problems. The National Allergy Bureau issues regional pollen reports, updated three times weekly, over the Internet (http://www.thriveonline.com/outdoors/go-guide/weather/pollen.usa.html); the reports include color-coded maps indicating pollen levels for trees, grasses, weeds, and molds.

Antihistamines, along with topical nasal steroid sprays, which are anti-inflammatory drugs that stop the allergic process, and prescription eye drops are the second line of defense for the allergy sufferer. Newer generation medicines are not only safer than earlier versions, but are vastly improved. Allergists stress that people who have abandoned medications in the past because they didn't work or produced side effects may want to reconsider. But be care-

Out of Breath?

Some people with allergies develop asthma, a potentially fatal condition caused by narrowing of the bronchial airways in the lungs that results in coughing, wheezing, and shortness of breath. Because cold, windy days can trigger an attack, early- and late-season hikers are particularly susceptible. Dr. Eric Schenkel, the director of asthma and allergy research at the Valley Clinical Research Center in Easton, Pennsylvania, recommends that asthma sufferers wear a scarf over their mouths when the mercury plummets, in order to keep the air they breathe moist and warm. If a trail companion has an asthma attack and has forgotten to pack an asthma inhaler, which can forestall the attack, Dr. Schenkel recommends that you try to keep the person calm and get him or her to drink a cup of strong, caffeinated coffee, which relaxes the constricted airways and can tide the person over until you reach medical help.

ful: Some over-the-counter allergy remedies have rebound effects, working for only a few days before symptoms roar back with a vengeance. Others can be dangerous for those with existing medical conditions or when taken in combination with other drugs. It's safest to consult an allergist before treating yourself with any medication.

Immunotherapy, or allergy shots, are reserved mainly for allergy sufferers who do not respond to other types of medications, or who are sensitive to so many substances that avoidance tactics and medications can't keep pace. However, hikers who have seasonal allergies that coincide with the times they want to be on the trail might also consider this type of treatment. Modern immunotherapy has a much higher success rate than it did a few years ago.

EYE CARE

Our eyes are among the most vulnerable organs in our bodies, but few hikers give any thought to protecting them from ultraviolet radiation or the tree branches and brush that overhang trails.

Anyone who does a lot of bushwhacking in thick cover should seriously consider buying glasses with clear, high-impact polycarbonate lenses for protection against corneal scratches. At high altitudes or in bright sunlight, it's important to wear lenses that offer 100 percent UV protection (polarized lenses cut glare from water and are nice if you plan to fish). Many retailers and catalogs offer sports glasses with interchangeable lenses to cover both bases.

Glacier glasses, which have a very dark tint and side shields to protect eyes from glare from snow and ice fields, are a must for winter hikers. I am sensitive on this subject because I once went snow-blind while backpacking in the winter and had to hike out by blinking one eye open for a split second, walking 10 feet with both eyes closed, and repeating the process for more than five miles before making it off the mountain.

Treatment

Dust, grit, and campfire sparks are among the leading causes of eye injuries. Immediately flush foreign particles out of the eye with water. If pain persists, the eye should be patched overnight. However, an eye that has become infected should not be patched. Sufferers of eye abrasions will be sensitive to direct sunlight for several days, but if pain persists for more than 24 hours, a foreign particle may have become embedded in the cornea and must be removed by a doctor.

Snow blindness, which is caused by sunburn of the eye's cornea, will almost always resolve within 24 to 48 hours, as long as the eyes are protected from sunlight.

CUTS AND LACERATIONS

In 99 percent of the lacerations caused by careless knife handling or other sharp objects, bleeding can be quickly controlled by applying direct pressure to the wound with the heel of your hand (apply sterile gauze, if possible) and elevating the limb. When bleeding stops, rinse the wound with clean water from your drinking container, gently flush or pick out any foreign debris, cleanse with an antibacterial wipe or peroxide, and apply a sterile gauze dressing. Puncture wounds caused by tree stubs, rusted nails, or other sharp objects do not drain freely and carry a high risk of infection. They should be cleaned and irrigated with disinfected water, but left open to heal.

Persistent bleeding that cannot be controlled by direct pressure can be slowed by applying pressure to major arteries. For arm wounds, press the brachial artery at the point where it crosses the upper arm bone on the inside of the arm. If a leg wound is bleeding profusely despite direct pressure and elevation, apply pressure to the femoral artery at the point where it crosses over the pelvic bone.

Most doctors stress that a tourniquet is a last resort, because by shutting off circulation, you risk tissue damage and possible amputation of the limb. When the femoral artery is severed—a rare occurrence in the backcountry but not unheard of (I know of several hunters who died when their knives slipped while they were dressing out deer)—there really isn't a choice. A tourniquet can be made with a shirt sleeve, pant leg, or a *wide* belt. Wrap the

---

Blood Blisters

A subungual hematoma, the accumulation of blood under a toenail or fingernail, is a common hiking injury sustained when a stone falls on your toe or when you miss while pounding a tent stake with a rock and smash your thumb or finger. To ease the pain and reduce swelling, make a small hole in the nail with a sharp knife point or a needle sterilized in a flame. A red-hot needle held with Leatherman-type pliers works well.

---

cloth above the wound and tie an overhand knot. Place a stick over the knot and tie another knot on top of it. Twist until the bleeding is controlled. Tie the loose ends of the cloth over the stick to keep it from unraveling. Whether to keep the tourniquet in place during evacuation is a controversial topic.

Some physicians recommend it; others advise loosening the tourniquet briefly every 10 or 15 minutes to check whether bleeding has stopped.

Treatment

Because sterile cleansing of wounds is next to impossible in the wilderness, some wilderness medical experts recommend that serious subcutaneous wounds or punctures be left open to prevent infection. The cavity should be cleansed as well as possible, then packed with a sterile gauze dressing that is changed daily. This is especially true of animal bites or wounds that have grit or dirt embedded in them.

Most minor cuts that can be cleaned thoroughly will heal more quickly if closed. Cleanse, apply an antibiotic or antiseptic ointment, and close with a butterfly bandage or skin-closure tape. Another option my brother recommends for minor lacerations of the extremities is Super Glue or, better yet, a special tissue glue made for wound closing. Press the sides of the cut together, apply a strip of Super Glue over the *surface* of the laceration and the skin on either side, and hold until it adheres. Bandage over top.

Scalp and facial wounds are less likely to become infected than wounds to other parts of the body and can be closed to minimize scarring. However, they first need to be cleansed, irrigated, and treated with an antibiotic or antiseptic ointment. *Any* serious wound that becomes infected must be reopened, cleansed, and packed open with sterile gauze until you reach a doctor.

BONE FRACTURES, DISLOCATIONS, AND SPRAINS

Bone fractures are serious injuries that need to be treated by a doctor. Be particularly careful with hikers who have had climbing mishaps. Spinal injuries resulting from falls can result in paralysis.

Treatment

Don't attempt to move any victim who has neck or back pain. If the victim is unconscious, keep the airway open by gripping the lower jaw and pulling forward away from the face. Do not bend the head or neck. Drape the victim with a sleeping bag and send one member of your party for help. As a general rule, it takes at least six adults to evacuate a seriously injured hiker from deep in the wilderness. Only attempt an evacuation if waiting for a rescue party will be of greater risk than moving the victim.

Collarbone and upper arm injuries should be splinted and/or placed in a sling to immobilize the limb. You can make a sling out of a shirt and improvise a splint from a stick, the plastic stay in a backpack, or even a rolled-up closed-cell foam pad. Fingers can be splinted with a pencil or piece of branch, or use the buddy system, taping the injured finger to its neighbor for added support. Use strips of cloth torn from a shirt to keep the splint in place. Do not risk cutting off circulation by wrapping it too tightly.

If you have taken a wilderness medicine course, you may attempt to reposition some types of bone fracture by applying pressure. Don't try this unless you know what you are doing. Immobilize the fracture by applying a makeshift splint fashioned from sticks, pack frames, closed-cell sleeping pads, or other semi-rigid objects, and immediately evacuate the victim.

By contrast, a dislocated joint should be "reduced" as quickly as possible to relieve pressure on the nerves and blood vessels. This is usually accomplished by applying pressure and traction until the joint is back in position. Because it can be difficult for untrained hikers to distinguish between fractures, sprains, and dislocations, some medical experts advise that the best course of action is simply to get the victim to qualified help. But if you know a little about reducing dislocations, you can save the victim a lot of agony and further injury by repositioning the joint. Many victims of shoulder dislocations are familiar with first aid treatments because they have had the problem before. Shoulder dislocations can be treated in the field (see illustration on next page).

Sprains are probably the most common hiking injuries and result when the ligaments around a joint become stretched and torn. Sometimes it is difficult to know whether the joint is sprained or broken. If there is a fracture, you may be able to feel and hear the bones grinding under the skin. You will not be able to walk on most fractures. But if you are within a day's hike of a trailhead or road, you probably can walk out on a sprained ankle. Don't dally deciding what to do. The initial excruciating pain of most sprains subsides enough in 10 to 15 minutes to allow you to walk. Keep your boot on and get going. Removing the boot and resting first will allow the ankle to swell and stiffen, making walking on it more difficult, and in the case of severe sprains, almost impossible.

Once you get home, or if you are days into the backcountry and must wait for the sprain to heal before leaving, treat with RICE: rest, ice (immersion in a cold creek will do), compression, and elevation. Cold helps reduce swelling, as does a compression bandage or wrap made from cloth. Keep the ankle above heart level while you rest and continue treating with cold water periodically. Most sprains, if rested at the outset of injury, will heal enough for you to walk gingerly on them in 48 hours. But it will take up to half a year for the damaged ligaments to completely regain their strength. You risk a permanent injury by testing them too soon.

To reset a dislocated shoulder, have the victim lie atop a log. Wrap a 10- to 15-pound stone inside a shirt and tie the sleeves to the victim's wrist. The stone should not touch the ground. When the muscles tire, the shoulder will slip back into place.

SHOCK

Shock is a serious condition brought about by traumatic injuries, such as a severe fall, lightning strike, or even snakebite. It can result in death unless immediate measures are taken to revive and stabilize the victim.

Treatment

Treating shock requires that the rescuer be familiar with the ABCs of field medicine: clear the **a**irway, check for **b**reathing, restore **c**irculation. It requires a working knowledge of cardiopulmonary resuscitation (CPR). The thumbnail description in this or any other manual is no substitute for becoming certified in CPR by the American Heart Association or the Red Cross. Anyone who spends much time outdoors where medical response is slow should sign up for a course. It will give you the breath of life should trail companions falter.

The three basic steps for reviving a person who has no discernible heartbeat and has stopped breathing are:

1. Place the victim on his back and open the airway by lifting the chin and removing any visible foreign debris from the mouth or throat with a finger sweep.

2. If the victim is still not breathing, inflate the lungs by pinching the nostrils, placing your lips around his or her mouth, and administering two full breaths.

3. Compress the chest by placing the heel of one hand against the sternum, the other hand on top of the first, and then pressing down sharply. Keep your shoulders directly over your hands and your elbows locked. Press at a rate of 80 compressions per minute. Do not compress an adult's

---

Backpacker's and Hiker's Medical Kit

- first aid booklet
- latex surgical gloves (non-latex gloves if you or others in your party are allergic to latex)
- adhesive strip bandages for minor cuts and scrapes
- 4″ × 4″ square sterile gauze pads (at least two, extra thick)
- tiny scissors or scalpel blade (for shaving calluses, draining abscesses, lancing blisters, cutting away dead skin)
- tweezers for splinters
- safety pins to secure elastic wrap or for fastening a sling
- sharp medical needle (for removing splinters, prickly pear spines, and so on)
- white athletic tape to stabilize sprained ankles and apply bandages
- antibacterial or iodine wipe
- soap-impregnated sponge for cleaning dirty wounds
- antibacterial ointment (Polysporin recommended)
- tincture of benzoin to rub on skin before applying adhesive tape or moleskin (it makes the adhesive stick better)
- moleskin and Spenco 2nd Skin for blisters
- wound-closure strips or butterfly bandages
- aspirin and acetaminophen (for fever, pain, headaches, altitude sickness, and so on)
- ibuprofen for fever, pain, and use as an anti-inflammatory
- antihistamine (diphenhydramine) tablets to relieve cold symptoms, allergic reactions and itching from poison ivy and insect bites
- Imodium for diarrhea
- antacid (Maalox, Mylanta, Tums)
- personal medications (such as epinephrine if someone in your party suffers from asthma or is allergic to bee stings)

chest more than two inches. After 15 seconds, administer two more breaths. Repeat until breathing and pulse are restored or until medical help arrives. (To perform CPR on children, you must increase the rate of compressions and alter the method of applying pressure, from heel of hand to fingers or thumbs. Pressing too hard can cause serious damage. A course will teach you how to administer CPR and wilderness first aid correctly.)

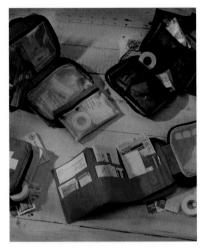

A small first aid kit should be carried in every hiker's pack.

A CAUTIONARY WORD

The thumbnail sketches of injuries and treatments in this chapter are incomplete. For example, I have not mentioned two forms of altitude sickness, high altitude pulmonary edema (HAPE) and high altitude cerebral edema (HACE), both of which can be fatal unless symptoms are recognized and the victim is properly treated and evacuated to a lower altitude. Nor have I discussed water rescues or the differences between treating a person suffering from hypothermia after cold water immersion and hypothermia from exposure to cold air. Acting on incomplete information can in some cases prove more damaging to the injured than not acting at all. However, I felt it was important to include this chapter because in most instances, some previous knowledge of symptoms and treatments will help the rescuer better attend those who are injured, and when you are several miles from a trailhead, trained medical personnel are in very short supply.

For more complete information on wilderness first aid, I highly recommend *Medicine for the Outdoors,* by Paul S. Auerbach, M.D. (The Lyons Press, 1999).

Understand, however, that no amount of reading is a substitute for completing a course in wilderness medicine. Only by acquiring first-hand instruction will you become fully qualified to attend medical emergencies in the field.

CHAPTER 11

The Next Step

"What does the mountain care?
Ah, but a man's reach should exceed his grasp,
Or what's a heaven for?"

ROBERT BROWNING

Some people will never be content with just climbing the mountain. They want to know what lies on the far side, and beyond the spine of the pines against the horizon, and the ridge after that. For them, the trail really never ends until the mountains fall to the plains or a bluff that meets the sea. Other backpackers may crave the experience of hiking through desert or visiting country that sleeps under a blanket of snow. And a few aren't satisfied with confining their hikes to our shores at all. They yearn to trek through the jungle in Belize, or a rhododendron forest on the shoulders of the Himalayas.

All of these people want to test themselves by taking backpacking to a different level, where the trails are a little longer, a little colder, or a little bit wilder.

LONG DISTANCE HIKING

Thru-hiking is a term used to describe long-distance backpacking. The most famous thru-hiking trails in the United States are the Appalachian Trail, which runs more than 2,000 miles from Georgia's Amicalola Falls State Park to Maine's Mount Katahdin; the Pacific Crest Trail, which follows the spine of coastal mountains from Canada to Mexico; and the Continental Divide Trail, which crests the Rockies from Alberta to Mexico. All demand a commitment of at least five months for completion. Hikers who cannot get away for that long often do these trails in segments, perhaps completing their journey years down the road. Other formidable hikes include the John Muir Trail in the Sierra Nevada (200 miles) and the Wonderland Trail (93 miles), which circumnavigates the immense snow-clad shoulders of Washington's Mount Rainier.

For some, thru-hiking offers both the greatest physical challenge and the greatest reward of backpacking. But don't undertake a journey like this lightly. Bear in mind that more than a quarter of the 1,200 or more hikers who start the Appalachian Trail each spring drop out after 30 miles, at the first place where the trail crosses a road.

If you still think you would like to try such a great adventure, keep in mind a number of factors. First, a thru-hike requires conditioning. You don't just heft a 60-pound pack and start on a 2,000-mile walk. You build up to it by taking progressively longer hikes, during which you fine-tune your gear as well as your body. It's also a good idea to break in two pairs of boots; you'll walk out from under the first pair before the trip is over.

For thru-hikers, the analogy of a backpacker as a man who carries his house on his back can be taken literally. These hikers may cover another 100 miles of trail before restocking with food.

Long trips require extensive planning. You must obtain the correct maps and consider the seasons. For example, the Pacific Crest Trail must be hiked south to north, or else you'd spend the first two months trudging through snow. Thru-hikers need to pay greater attention to their calorie count and eat more to keep up their weight and energy than weekend warriors. Because a one week's supply of food weighs from 14 to 18 pounds, you'll have to re-stock every 8 to 10 days (for well-conditioned hikers, that translates to roughly 100 miles of trail). Most thru-hikers restock by mailing boxes of sup-plies to themselves, care of General Delivery, to post offices in towns near the trail. Others carry money to buy supplies or arrange to have them brought to pre-arranged destinations.

When planning a thru-hike, make the effort to contact clubs where mem-bers have first-hand experience. They can tell you where to leave packages and point out idiosyncrasies of the trails that can prove invaluable. A list of hiking clubs, as well as books that emphasize thru-hiking, are listed in Refer-ences at the back of the book.

WINTER CAMPING

I learned my first lesson about winter backpacking the hard way. After my wife and I had hiked over a deep snowpack into California's Sequoia National Park and pitched camp, we set our boots beside our sleeping bags before turning in. The following morning we awoke to discover that the boots had frozen as solidly as cement. We had to hold them over the flames of our cook-stove to soften the leather.

I brought back another nugget of wisdom from that ordeal as well. At least in northern latitudes, days are short and if you don't have a good book, a warm fire, or someone to talk to, then you are in for a very long night.

Winter hiking is work. You'll need to carry more clothing, a heavier sleep-ing bag, and a more substantial tent than you do in the summer. You may need special gear in the way of snow shovels, ice crampons, snowshoes, or cross-country skis. You won't travel as far in a day, but your pack will be heav-ier. You'll need to eat more and pack cheeses, nuts, and other foods rich in fat content, to generate warmth and energy over the long haul.

Survival skills are crucial. In the summer, you might be able to get away with becoming lost, falling into a creek, or having inadequate clothing and gear, and still live to tell your story. In the same country during winter you could develop hypothermia and end up in fine print on page two of the news-paper.

With such dangers, plus the rigors of winter camping, the natural question is, Why do it? I could cite a few practical reasons: summer crowds are gone, backcountry permits in the parks are easier to come by, and it's a good way to beat cabin fever and catch the sun, however few hours there may be of it. But these don't explain the allure of an alpine basin glistening under a blanket of snow, or the sound of a creek whispering underneath ice. Only in winter can one know the profound silence of a boreal forest or the diamond brilliance of the night sky—the serenity and solitude that are winter's glory.

Winter backpackers burn lots of energy. To restoke the furnace, this adventurer in British Columbia's Dogtooth Mountains may need to eat a couple of freeze-dried meals.

Winter Camping Tips

- Use ski poles for balance and climbing even if you aren't wearing skis or snowshoes. A ski pole with the webbing removed can be used as an emergency avalanche probe in case a companion is buried.

- Air out damp clothing and sleeping bags often and spend every fourth or fifth day in camp, resting up and drying your kit.

- To keep boots and gaiters pliable, stuff them into plastic bags and bring them into your sleeping bag at night.

- Use wide-necked water bottles. The mouth won't freeze as quickly as a narrow-necked container.

- Keep water from freezing by insulating it among bulky gear inside your pack during the day. Then wrap your container in a plastic bag and stuff it inside the sleeping bag at night.

- Keep your fuel bottle inside your sleeping bag, too. Fuel burns more efficiently when it is warm.

- Consider packing a lightweight thermos. Boil water at night, keep the thermos in your sleeping bag, and in the morning you can eat

Avalanche!

Next to hypothermia, the greatest danger of winter backcountry travel is avalanche. Never hike alone above timberline. Become familiar with the conditions that precipitate avalanches—namely, hard cornices of snow on lee slopes or a hard crust over an unstable snowpack on a slope between 30 and 50 degrees. It doesn't take deep snow to create avalanche conditions. An elk hunter hiking in 18 inches of snow south of my home died last year when the slope he was traversing began to slide.

Carry avalanche beepers and if you must cross a slope, trail 30 feet of brightly colored avalanche cord that is tied to your parka. Should you be buried, part of the cord may remain visible to direct your companions in their rescue effort.

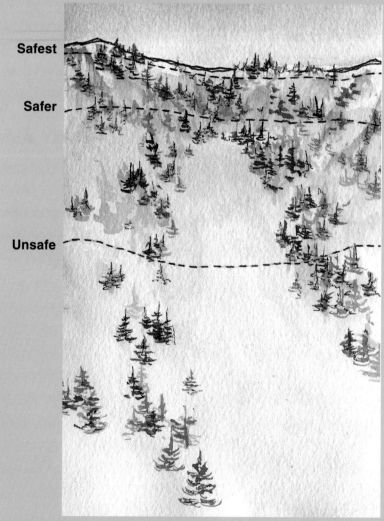

Safest

Safer

Unsafe

Avalanche danger is greatest on open slopes of snow that fall at a 30- to 50-degree angle. To be safe, cross through the timber well above the lowest dotted line or walk the ridge.

hot oatmeal and drink cocoa without ever getting out of your sleeping bag.

- Don't make the mistake of closing your tent too tightly. Without adequate ventilation, condensation from your breath and body heat will coat your sleeping bag and the tent walls with frost.

- Use a pair of plastic bags as slippers if you have to step outside the tent to urinate in the middle of the night.

- Bring extra batteries for your flashlight or a candle light for reading. During long nights, you will need much more illumination than you would in summer.

DESERT HIKING AND BACKPACKING

Our arid Southwest provides intrepid hikers an opportunity of traveling through a world of unique beauty. Great desert and canyon hiking areas include the Joshua Tree Monument in southern California, Arizona's Grand Canyon and Organ Pipe Cactus National Monument, and Utah's Zion National Park and Escalante Canyon.

By far the most comfortable seasons to hike through southern deserts are in winter and again in the spring, when cactus and wildflowers erupt in bloom. During the hotter months, it's wise to time desert and canyon hikes for the early morning or evening hours. By doing this, not only will you avoid the hottest part of the day, but you have a much better chance of observing native wildlife, for nearly all animals adapt to hot, arid environments by confining their movements to night and the bracketing hours of fading light. Remember to watch for snakes.

Desert Survival

In the desert, all other considerations for surviving pale in comparison to the importance of conserving and finding water.

Four liters is the minimum amount of fluid your body will require during a long dayhike. The water will sit like a stone in your pack (an 8-pound stone, to be precise), but could save your life should you become lost. Sip water at regular intervals, rather than only during a few rest stops. It can be absorbed better in small quantities. When backpacking, carry at least a two-day supply at all times and know beforehand exactly where you can find *reliable* water sources. Do not rely upon springs marked on topographic maps. Many are seasonally dry and others will have disappeared since the last geological survey.

In the desert, the source of water is the earth itself. Fine soils retain moisture months after rains have passed and this can be coaxed to the surface with a solar still (see illustration below). To make a still, you need a six-foot square tarp made from clear plastic, similar to the one recommended in Chapter 2 for building emergency shelters in cold climates, and a container to catch the water. A 4-foot long section of plastic hose, such as an aquarium hose, is optional. You need a fine-grain soil and a site that is open to direct sunlight.

As solar energy passes through the plastic and heats the soil, water in the soil evaporates, condenses on the bottom of the sheet and runs in droplets downhill, where it drips into the container. You can suck it up in the plastic tube. To increase the yield of a solar still, cut up sections of cactus to expose the moist insides and line the bottom of the hole with them.

Production can vary from less than one quart to about 3 quarts per still, per day.

To make a solar still, dig a concave hole in soil open to sunlight. Place a clear plastic tarp over the hole, holding the sides down with mounded up soil or sand. Place a stone in the center of the sheet. The hole should be deep enough to hold a water container with several inches clearance between the container and the sheet. As the earth heats, condensation will form on the bottom of the sheet. The water droplets will run to the center and drop into the container. Suck up water with a plastic hose.
(Note: For greater yield, line the bottom of the hole with chopped cactus or other vegetation.)

BACKPACKING OVERSEAS

The world is laced with great hiking trails, from the staggeringly gorgeous Milford Track, a 35-mile path through the New Zealand mountains, to the Coast to Coast Walk in the Lake District of northern England, to the Haute Route, which traverses the European Alps. You can even circumnavigate Africa's Mount Kenya on backpacking trails. What a great way to meet fellow adventurers and immerse yourself in foreign culture, and all for little more than the cost of a plane ticket.

No matter where you want to hike, the first trail you need to follow is the trail of information other travelers have left behind. Some useful guidebooks for foreign travel are listed in the References section at the back of this book. Hiking clubs are another good source of information. The Appalachian Mountain Club and the Sierra Club, for example, both offer outfitted treks on foreign soils and have a warehouse of information for do-it-yourselfers. Commercial outfitters are a good source of information once you've narrowed the possibilities to specific destinations.

Make sure to arrange passports and visas well ahead of your trip. Visa requirements can be confusing, so it's best to contact the U.S. State De-

Travel Tips

- Zip your backpack in a duffel bag before checking it at the airport. Luggage handlers are rough on backpacks, and exposed pockets are an inviting target for thieves.
- Keep valuables, including your money, passport, and a return plane ticket in either a money belt or a beltpack that you wear at all times.
- Make two photocopies of your passport. Keep one in your baggage, separate from the original, and leave the third at home. They will facilitate getting a new passport should the original become lost or stolen.
- Carry several passport-sized photographs of yourself. They will come in handy if you need to apply for an unexpected visa, lose your passport, or are faced with an emergency.
- Consider buying insurance to avoid possible huge rescue bills in case you get lost or hurt in a remote area.
- Bring iodine tablets and purify all but bottled water.
- Don't count on being able to purchase the correct film for your camera. Bring more rolls than you think you'll need, as well as a spare camera battery. Bring extra batteries for flashlights, GPS units, or any other gear.
- Bring a repair kit for your tent, stove, and inflatable mattress.
- Pack a multifuel stove if you will be camping in Third World countries. Coleman fuel and unleaded gasoline may be difficult to find, but kerosene is almost universally available.

partment (phone 202–647–5225), which publishes information specific to almost any country you may want to visit. The State Department also is a good starting point for inquiring about safety and medical alerts in different parts of the world. For information on vaccine requirements, call the federal Centers for Disease Control (404–639–2537).

The High Life

In some foreign lands, the concept of backpacking is loosely defined. Long-distance trekkers may indeed carry packs, but at night they stay in dormitories or huts near the trail. You can hike from hut to hut through the peaks of the Dolomites in Italy, through the nirvana of New Zealand's South Island backcountry, through England and Wales, even through Japan's North Alps. In fact, along some of the world's most spectacular alpine trails in Europe and New Zealand, camping en route is not permitted, in order to preserve the fragile ecosystems.

Staying in huts can bump up the cost of a backpacking trip, but the trade-off of being able to sleep with a roof over your head and perhaps take a shower is one many hikers are more than willing to make. And staying in communal shelters and dorms is a great way to meet other intrepid adventurers, which for many hikers is as rewarding as seeing the sights.

Staying in shelters provides an attractive alternative for people who want to experience long-distance hiking, but are uncomfortable sleeping outdoors or carrying 50-pound packs up a mountainside. It is a way of having your cake and eating it, too.

To intrepid hikers, even the Himalayas are fair game. But the first trail to follow for overseas travel is the trail of information others have left behind.

AFTERWORD

The Freedom of the Trail

"To myself I sometimes appear as a wild Indian or an old Berserker, masquerading under the guise of a 19th-century American. When the straightjacket of civilization becomes too oppressive, I throw it off, betake myself to savagery, and there loaf and refresh my soul."

GEORGE WASHINGTON SEARS ("NESSMUK")

Liberty is a word to which Americans attach great political significance. But are we truly free? Or are we bound by the straitjacket of civilization to a greater degree than we wish to admit?

Nessmuk, so christened by Native Americans who recognized the kindred soul of a wanderer, escaped 19th-century oppressions with the paddle of his canoe into New York's Adirondack Mountains. This book has been written for those who make an escape on their feet, but whose purpose—to roam freely and refresh their spirits in nature—remains unchanged more than a century later.

As I was completing the final chapter of the book, my belief in the importance of wild country as a ticket to freedom was put to the test. My teenage son and daughter, along with their cousin Christy and two friends, decided to end the summer by taking a backpacking trip into Wyoming's Beartooth Mountains. In another week they would be returning to the prison of our educational institutions, and this, they insisted, was their last chance to break free from the bonds of obligation and parental supervision that had dogged them all summer long.

Wilderness is another word for freedom. By protecting undeveloped lands, we pass down a heritage of opportunity for our children, so that their spirits too may soar.

My wife and I feared for their safety. At 19, Christy was a fairly experienced driver, but even after negotiating the hairpin bends that climb to the Beartooth Plateau, they would have to carry heavy packs at more than 10,000-feet elevation, in a season when arrows of lightning shivered on the horizon every afternoon. Not to mention the grizzly bears.

But in the end we relinquished them to the gods like all parents must, and they drove off with what hodgepodge of backpacking gear I could dredge from our basement. The irony of having just completed an instructional book on the subject of their journey rested heavily on my soul. I had put all my years of experience into black and white, yet had sent novices on their way with outdated equipment and only a few words of advice. Still, hadn't I wandered at even a younger age, with not so much as a match in my pocket? And had not that freedom enriched my soul? But then, that was in Ohio.

A couple of days passed, during which I thought of all the things that might go wrong. When twilight turned to darkness on the evening they were scheduled to return, I called my wife, who was working late, and we worried a while together. I hung up the phone, knowing the feeling of the empty nest that would be ours in only a few short years. A heartbeat later the door opened. And there they were, their faces aglow with windburn by the light of the porch lamp, their excitement bubbling over.

Breathlessly, they told me their story. The first mishap had been a wrong turn, and that had been before ever leaving town. Their next mistake was running on empty up the grade to the Beartooths. They had siphoned gas from a charitable motorist, splashing a pint or two onto their clothes in the process. High on fumes, but with enough fuel in the tank to carry on, they had sailed right on by the road to the trailhead and had driven for an hour before realizing their mistake. By the time they turned back, there was barely enough light to hike five miles to the lake.

The next day the skies opened and they had to spend the entire day loafing and refreshing their souls, while hail, sleeting rain, and snow pelted the rain fly over their heads. When the rain stopped, they tried and failed to build a fire. Attempting to cook a late brunch on a one-burner stove, they melted several plastic forks trying to flip pancakes that would not hold a shape; they ended up eating them like mush out of cupped hands. To everyone's chagrin, they discovered they had brought no toilet paper.

That evening they were so cold that all five crammed into a three-man tent for warmth. To regain circulation in their feet and hands, which had begun to turn blue, they held "worm wars," where everybody zipped up in their sleeping bags with their arms inside and their hoods over their heads and bounded about like kangaroos, knocking each other down and rolling around. They played cards until two in the morning. They all got irritable; they accused each other of cheating; they had

By offering us a bridge to exploration, hiking and backpacking expand the borders of our earth, as well as the horizons of our minds.

Hiking in the High Sierra just outside Yosemite National Park.

but one pillow and stole it back and forth until dawn. What snatches of sleep they did manage were interrupted by a mountain goat nibbling at the corners of the tent. Yet when the sun shone in the morning, so did their spirits rise, and they hiked back to the car to discover that the hardships had solidified their camaraderie and they were all fast friends.

Christy summed up the trip this way: "Everybody survived; nobody was arrested."

It was, by everyone's account, a grand adventure. It wasn't a backpacking adventure by the book—not by this book, anyway. But perhaps that's the point. If every step of a hike or every leg of a backpacking trip goes exactly as planned, wherein lies the adventure?

That is something to keep in mind the next time the tent leaks or the bear finds your bear hang to be not so bearproof, after all. The greatest rewards in life are often gifts of the unexpected. And the last realm of the unexpected lies beyond the road's end, along the liberty of the trail.

SECTION III

REFERENCES

Appendix

CLOTHING CHECKLISTS

Hot Weather Clothing

- synthetic undershorts and T-shirt
- cotton or nylon shorts or zip-off pants
- cotton, polyester or polyester/nylon-blend shirt
- broad-brimmed hat
- bandanna to dip in water for evaporative cooling
- synthetic sports-blend socks

Mountain Clothing

- synthetic undershorts
- lightweight, synthetic undershirt and long johns
- synthetic zip-off pants or tights
- chamois, microfleece or wool shirt
- fleece jacket
- waterproof/breathable rain jacket and pants
- lightweight fleece gloves
- ball cap and fleece or wool hat

- silk scarf or fleece neck gaiter
- synthetic sports-blend socks or polypropylene liner socks with wool-blend outer sock

Rainy Day Clothing

(in addition to appropriate synthetic clothing for the temperature)

- waterproof/breathable rain jacket and pants
- poncho
- waterproof gaiters
- extra socks

Winter Clothing

- synthetic undershorts
- midweight polyester long underwear, top and bottom
- midweight wool or fleece pants
- wool or microfleece shirt
- fleece jacket
- down vest
- fleece or wool balaclava
- oversize parka
- gaiters
- silk scarf or fleece neck gaiter
- polypropylene sock liners and wool or fleece outer socks

HIKER'S EMERGENCY KIT

(for zippered belt pouch or daypack)

- waterproof matches
- butane cigarette lighter
- flint and steel
- solid fuel cubes or other fire-starting material

- plumber's candle
- emergency space blanket (the kind that is sewn in the shape of a sleeping bag is the most efficient at conserving body warmth)
- 2 compasses
- sunscreen
- small medical kit (many outdoor stores sell these, or they can be mail-ordered through L.L. Bean)
- Spenco 2nd Skin blister kit
- personal medications
- iodine tablets for water purification
- flashlight with spare bulb and batteries (wrap the barrel with a few turns of electrical tape and a few turns of duct tape that can be used for repairs)
- signal mirror
- shrill whistle
- 10 feet of bright orange marking tape to mark a trail in case you become lost
- knife
- roll of dental floss with a heavy-duty needle taped inside the lid*
- folded square of aluminum foil†
- trail bar

Optional Additions to Emergency Kit

- trail guide
- topographic map and pencil to plot compass courses
- emergency strobe, smoke bomb, or signal flare to alert rescuers of your position in event of injury or becoming lost
- Sawyer Extractor, a suction device that can remove snake venom from the source of the bite, reducing necrotic tissue damage
- 6-foot square of clear plastic Visqueen or coated nylon tarp

---

*Dental floss makes an excellent strong thread; I once used to it to stitch up my wife's pack after a bear had ripped it apart while we were backpacking in Yosemite National Park.

†Foil has a dozen and one uses, including catching rainwater, cooking trout, covering a cup or pot, or even providing a heat-reflecting foundation to build an emergency fire on in snow country.

- lightweight folding saw
- nylon cord (30–50 feet of parachute "550" cord)
- insect repellent
- cayenne pepper spray (for country where bear encounters are common)

BASIC BACKPACKING CHECKLIST

- backpack
- shelter (tarp or tent)
- sleeping bag
- sleeping pad
- 12-inch square of closed-cell pad (for sitting on in camp and during rest stops)
- cookstove and accessories (fuel container, funnel, windscreen, priming paste, eye dropper)
- pot and pot grabber or handle
- cup/mug
- plate/bowl
- spoon
- dish scrubber
- food bag
- pocket knife or multipurpose tool
- 50 feet of nylon cord (550 parachute cord)
- poncho
- emergency kit
- flashlight wrapped with duct tape (either Mini-MagLite with headband or Bite-Lite accessory for holding it between your teeth, or headlamp)
- extra flashlight batteries and spare bulb
- medical kit and foot care items
- wide-necked 1-liter water bottle
- collapsible water bag
- water purification system (either iodine tablets or filter pump)

- sunglasses
- insect repellent
- map
- toilet trowel and toilet paper
- notebook, pencil
- plastic garbage bags (several sizes)
- toothbrush and toothpaste

Checklist Recommendations for Extended Trips

- camp shoes (either lightweight athletic shoes, sandals, or "aqua shoes" for wading and lazing about camp)
- stove repair kit
- self-inflating foam mattress repair kit
- knife sharpener
- paperback book
- playing cards

Checklist Options for Hiking/Backpacking

- backpack cover (rainy country)
- hiking staff or walking sticks
- clear plastic tarp for solar still (desert hiking)
- cayenne pepper spray (in bear country)
- camera
- fishing equipment
- field guides (to wildflowers, reptiles, birds, etc.)
- notepad and pencil
- binoculars
- collection net

Backpacker's Repair Kit

- needle and strong thread or dental floss
- duct tape

- patch kit for self-inflating mattress
- extra parts for stove
- Super Glue
- sleeve for broken tent pole
- multipurpose tool or Swiss Army knife

FOOD CHECKLISTS

Breakfast

- instant oatmeal (2 packets per day)
- dry cereal (granola, Muesli)
- dried milk
- coffee, cocoa, tea
- ramen noodle sup/Cup-A-Soup

Lunch/Trail Food

- trail mix
- jerky
- cheese
- pepperoni stick
- dried fruit
- nuts
- pita (pocket) bread
- granola bars
- Kudos
- trail bars
- fresh fruit treats
- peanut butter
- bagels
- crackers

Dinner

- instant soup as first course (ramen noodles, miso, Knorr and Lipton fancy soups)

- freeze-dried meals
- instant mashed potatoes
- instant rice
- macaroni and cheese
- pasta
- couscous
- stuffing mix
- small cans of beef/chicken/oysters/fish/meat spread/TVP (textured vegetable protein)

Condiments and Spices

- dried herbs (oregano, thyme, marjoram, chives, basil)
- powdered spices (curry, garlic, onion)
- Parmesan cheese
- chicken and beef boullion cubes
- dried mushrooms
- dried tomatoes
- tamari or soy sauce
- miso packet
- mustard
- honey
- clarified butter (unclarified butter will spoil more quickly)
- salt
- pepper

BACKCOUNTRY MEDICAL KIT

- latex surgical gloves
- mouth shield/mask for rescue breathing
- adhesive-strip bandages for minor cuts and scrapes
- 4″ × 4″ square sterile gauze pads (at least 2)
- scissors or scalpel blade (for shaving calluses, draining abscesses, lancing blisters, cutting away dead skin)
- tweezers for splinters

- safety pins to secure elastic wrap
- medical needle (for removing splinters, prickly pear spines, etc.)
- white athletic tape to stabilize sprained ankles and apply bandages
- antibacterial or iodine wipe
- soap-impregnated sponge for cleaning dirty wounds
- antibacterial ointment (Polysporin recommended)
- tincture of benzoin to rub on skin before applying adhesive tape or moleskin (it makes adhesives stick better)
- moleskin and Spenco 2nd Skin for blisters
- wound-closure strips or butterfly bandages
- Super Glue (for closing minor lacerations)
- aspirin and acetaminophen (for fever, pain, headaches, altitude sickness, etc.)
- Motrin or ibuprofen (for fever, pain, and use as an anti-inflammatory)
- antihistamine tablets (to relieve cold symptoms, allergic reactions, and itching from poison ivy and insect bites)
- Imodium for diarrhea
- antacid (Maalox, Mylanta, Tums)
- personal medications
- beesting kit for allergy sufferers
- first aid booklet
- coins or phone card

Sources

EQUIPMENT AND CLOTHING

L.L. Bean offers a complete selection of hiking, camping and backpacking gear, as well as boots and outdoor clothing. Selections range from practical, inexpensive gear to the most innovative designs. The staff will be happy to help you choose equipment to fit your family's needs and budget, and all merchandise is unconditionally guaranteed. To place an order or request a catalog, call 1-800-221-4221. You can shop on-line at *www.llbean.com*. The L.L. Bean store, located in Freeport, Maine, is a New England landmark. Built in 1912, it is open 24 hours a day, 365 days a year.

Two other suppliers that offer a full range of products include:

- Recreational Equipment, Inc. (REI)
  P.O. Box 1938
  Sumner, WA 98390
  1-800-426-4840

- Cabela's
  One Cabela Drive
  Sidney, NE 69160
  1-800-237-4444

OUTDOOR SCHOOLS

L.L. Bean's Outdoor Discovery Schools offer instruction in backpacking, ca-
noeing, kayaking, flyfishing, wilderness first aid, outdoor photography, wing
shooting, mountain biking, bushwhacking and navigation with map and
compass, with special programs for children and for parents with children.
For information, call 1-800-341-4341, ext. 26666, or write to the L.L. Bean
Outdoor Discovery Schools, Freeport, ME 04033.

Other well-respected outdoor schools include:

- Outward Bound
  R.R. 2, Box 280
  Garrison, NY 10524-9757
  1-914-424-4000

- NOLS, the National Outdoor Leadership Schools
  288 Main St.
  Lander, WY 82520
  1-307-332-8800

Contact NOLS for information on the *Leave No Trace* principles for backcountry use. Or phone *Leave No Trace* at 1-800-332-4100 to obtain booklets for
wise outdoor use specific to the region you intend to visit.

CONSERVATION ORGANIZATIONS

These conservation organizations sponsor many outdoor education programs, and offer superlative publications and activities, including organized
hiking trips.

- National Wildlife Federation (NWF)
  1400 16th St. NW
  Washington, DC 20036
  1-202-797-6800

Members may receive a subscription to *Ranger Rick*, an excellent wildlife magazine for children.

- Nature Conservancy
  1815 N. Lynn St.
  Arlington, VA 22209
  1-703-841-5300

- Sierra Club
  85 Second St. (2nd floor)
  San Francisco, CA 94105
  1-415-977-5500

- Wilderness Society
  900 17th St. NW
  Washington, DC 20006
  1-202-833-2300

HIKING ORGANIZATIONS

- American Hiking Society
  1422 Fenwick Lane
  Silver Springs, MD 20910
  1-301-565-6704

- Appalachian Mountain Club
  5 Joy St.
  Boston, MA 02108
  1-617-523-0636

The AMC maintains a database of hiking clubs throughout the United States. Contact them to locate a club in the area you wish to visit.

THRU-HIKING ASSOCIATIONS

- Appalachian Trail Conference
  P.O. Box 807
  Harpers Ferry, WV 25425
  www.atconf.org

- Continental Divide Trail Alliance
  P.O. Box 628
  Pine, CO 80470

- Pacific Crest Trail Association
  5325 Elkhorn Boulevard Suite 256
  Sacramento, CA 95842

BOOKS
Hiking and Backpacking

- *Walking Magazine's Complete Guide to Walking for Health, Fitness, and Weight Loss,* by Mark Fenton. The Lyons Press, 2000.
- *The Complete Walker III,* by Colin Fletcher. Alfred A. Knopf, 1984. Fletcher, an erudite, transplanted Welshman is windy, opinionated, and irreverent. Although some gear recommendations are out-of-date, *The Complete Walker* remains the "bible" on backpacking and is an excellent sourcebook, as well as providing highly entertaining reading.
- *L.L. Bean Family Camping Handbook,* by Keith McCafferty. The Lyons Press, 1999.
- *Hiking and Backpacking,* by Karen Berger. A Trailside Guide. W.W. Norton and Co., 1995.
- *The Dayhiker's Handbook,* by John Long and Michael Hodgson. Ragged Mountain Press, 1996.
- *The Backpacker's Handbook,* by Chris Townsend. Ragged Mountain Press, 1997.
- *The National Outdoor Leadership School's Wilderness Guide,* by Mark Harvey. Simon and Schuster, 1999.
- *The Outward Bound Backpacker's Handbook,* by Glenn Randall. The Lyons Press, 2000.

Thru-Hiking, Winter Backpacking, Desert Hiking, Hiking in Foreign Lands

- *Advanced Backpacking,* by Karen Berger. A Trailside Guide. W.W. Norton and Co., 1998.
- *Winterwise: A Backpacker's Guide,* by John M. Dunn. Adirondack Mountain Club, 1989.
- *AMC Guide To Winter Camping,* by Steven Gorman. Appalachian Mountain Club, 1991.
- *Desert Hiking,* by Dave Ganci. Wilderness Press, 1993.
- *Long Distance Hiking,* by Ronald Mueser. Ragged Mountain Press, 1998.

Backpack Cooking

- *Backcountry Cooking* (from Backpacker Magazine), by Dorcas S. Miller. The Mountaineers, 1998.

- *The Well-Fed Backpacker,* by June Fleming. Random House, 1986.
- *Simple Foods for the Pack,* by Claudia Axcell, et al. Sierra Club, 1986.

Hiking and Backpack Guidebooks

- *Falcon Guides.* Falcon Publishing, P.O. Box 1718, Helena, Mt. 59624. One of the best series guides, books cover many states as well as specific natural areas.
- *Foghorn Press series.* Foghorn Press, P.O. Box 2036, Santa Rosa, CA 95405.
- *Trail Guide series.* Trail Guide Books, P.O. Box 148, Weiser, ID 83672.
- *100 Hikes series.* The Mountaineers, 1001 SW Klickitat Way, Seattle, WA 98134.
- *Johnson Books series.* Johnson Printing, 1880 S. 57h Court, Boulder, CO 80301
- *50 Hikes series.* Countryman Press, Box 748, Woodstock, VT 05091
- *Lonely Planet.* A series of guides for trekking abroad. Lonely Planet Publications, 150 Linden St., Oakland, CA 94607.

Navigation

- *The Outward Bound Map & Compass Handbook,* by Glenn Randall. The Lyons Press, 1998.
- *Wilderness Navigation: Finding Your Way Using Map, Compass, Altimiter and GPS,* by Bob Burns and Mike Burns. The Mountaineers, 1999.
- *GPS Made Easy,* by Lawrence Letham. The Mountaineers, 1995.
- *Staying Found: The Complete Map & Compass Handbook,* by June Fleming. The Mountaineers, 1994.
- *The Essential Wilderness Navigator,* by David Seidman. Ragged Mountain Press, 1995.

Wilderness Survival Manuals

- *Mountaineering: Freedom of the Hills,* edited by Don Graydon. The Mountaineers, 1991.
- *Wilderness Skiing and Winter Camping,* by Chris Townsend. Ragged Mountain Press, 1994.

- *Emergency Survival Handbook,* by Robert E. Brown. American Outdoor Safety League.

Wilderness Medical Guides

- *Medicine for the Outdoors,* by Paul A. Auerbach, M.D. The Lyons Press, 1999. "By far the best book on the subject."—*Field & Stream*
- *Commonsense Outdoor Medicine and Emergency Companion,* by Newell Breyfogle. Ragged Mountain Press, 1994. A good pocket-size guide.
- *Pocket Guide to Wilderness Medicine & First Aid,* by Paul G. Gill, Jr., M.D. Ragged Mountain Press, 1997.
- *NOLS Wilderness First Aid,* by Tod Schimelpfenig and Linda Lindsey. Stackpole Books, 1992.

MAGAZINES

- *Backpacker.* Rodale Press, Inc. Annual equipment guide, product testing, and gear reviews are especially helpful.
- *Outside.* Mariah Media Inc. A mix of outdoor adventure and travel. Look for annual gear review.

MAPS

You can order United States Geological Survey quad maps for any area by phoning the Earth Science Information Center: (800) USA-MAPS. Or order by writing:

- U.S. Geological Survey
  Box 25286 Denver Federal Center
  Denver, CO 80225
- *Trails Illustrated* (series)
  P.O. Box 3610
  Evergreen, CO 80439
  1-800-962-1643
- *The Map Catalogue,* edited by Jack McKower. Vintage Books. Random House, 1992. An extensive reference work for maps worldwide.

- *Delorme Atlas/Gazetteer* (series and U.S.G.S. maps on CD-ROM)
  P.O. Box 298
  Yarmouth, ME 04096
  1-207-846-7000
  www.delorme.com

- Navitrak (U.S.G.S. maps on CD-ROM)
  603 Argus Road, Suite 201
  Oakville, Ontario
  Canada L6J6GS
  1-800-257-6766
  www.navitrak.com

- Maptech, Inc. (maps on CD-ROM)
  1 Riverside Drive
  Andover, MA 01810-1122
  1-978-933-3000
  www.maptech.com

INTERNET ACCESS

At the time of writing, these are a few of the most useful Web sites for hiking
and backpacking reference:

- GORP—Great Outdoor Recreation Page. This reference includes links to
  hiking and backpacking throughout the United States, as well as in
  Europe, New Zealand and other foreign countries)
  www.gorp.com

- Backpacker Magazine
  www.backpacker.com

- Hiking and Walking Home Page
  www.teleport.com/~walking/hiking.html

- Dayhiking
  www.dayhiker.com

- Backpacking Home Page
  www.thebackpacker.com

- Hikenet: Your Virtual Trail on the Web
  http://members.aol.com/hikenet/index.html

- Trailplace (Appalachian Trail Thru-hikers' Link)
  www.trailplace.com

- Yahoo Hiking Reference Page
  www.yahoo.com/Entertainment/Outdoor/Hiking
- Outside Magazine
  www.outsidemag.com
- American Hiking Society
  www.americanhiking.org
- Hiking and Camping
  www.greatoutdoors.com/hiking/
- Appalachian Mountain Club Home Page
  www.amc-nh.org
- Mountain Zone
  www.mountainzone.com/hike
- Trail Walking
  www.trailwalk.com
- Hiking Trails and Backpacking Trip Planning Information
  www.trailweb.com
- Hiking the Continental Divide Trail
  www.cdtrail.org

Fishing in the Wind River Range.

Photo Credits

Acknowledgments

My sixteen-year-old son Tom provided the watercolor illustrations for this book. He is a gifted artist and I would like to thank him for taking time from his summer vacation to help me with this project.

The miles would have seemed a lot longer were it not for the companions with whom I have had the pleasure of sharing a trail. My father was the first by my side. My mother followed in shoes that should have never left pavement, to warn me to stay out of the poison ivy. My brother, Kevin, was the co-conspirator with whom I disappeared from sight from Maine to Montana, much to our parents' consternation.

I'd also like to remember my wonderful childhood friend, Karen Basil, who accompanied me on countless snake-catching expeditions into briar jungles and rock cliffs we both would have been wiser to avoid.

Others who have illuminated woodland paths include Randy Mervis, Bill Morris, Bruce Milnes, Dean McNeil, Bob and Duncan Bullock, Bo Bullock, Robert Mussey, Gigi Wilson, Drick Boyd, Laura Ceperly, Bob Gillett, Dolores Garcia, Joe Gutkoski, Mel Kotur, Cathy Myers, Claude Chateau, Bill Basil, Carly and Trevor Basil, Luke Bovenizer, Bob and Jamie Schontzler, my wife, Gail, and a very long string of children, including, most importantly, my son, Tom, and daughter, Jessie.

Special thanks go to Steve and Dale Dunn, who took the pen out of my hand and replaced it with something better, and to my brother, Kevin, an emergency room physician, who lent his expertise on wilderness maladies. I'd also like to acknowledge Dr. Paul Auerbach, who checked the chapter on illness and injury for accuracy.

And thanks again to Bryan Oettel, Jill Hindle, Tony Lyons, and Nick Lyons at the Lyons Press, as well as all the folks at L.L. Bean for making this book possible.

Index